Resolving Conflict

Improving Communication

Resolving Conflict

Improving Communication

A Guide for Healthcare Professionals

The Honourable Judge Heather A. Lamoureux

Elaine Seifert, Q.C.

Medical editing by Tanis Blench, M.D., M.B.A.
and Brian D. Stewart, M.D., FRCPC

Kingsley
PUBLISHING

Cover and interior design by Dpict Visual Communications

Project management by Kingsley Publishing Services
www.kingsleypublishing.ca

Printed in Canada by Friesens

2009 / 1

Library and Archives Canada Cataloguing in Publication

Lamoureux, Heather
    Resolving conflict & improving communication : a guide for healthcare professionals /
Heather A. Lamoureux, Elaine Seifert ; medical editing by Tanis Blench and Brian D. Stewart.

Includes bibliographical references and index.
ISBN 978-0-9784526-3-6

    1. Communication in medicine. 2. Conflict management. 3. Medical personnel and patient.
4. Medical care. I. Siefert, Elaine II. Title. III. Title: Resolving conflict and improving communication.

R728.L34 2009   610.69'6   C2009-902027-0

Ordering information: www.kingsleypublishing.ca

Disclaimer: All scenarios, names, and situations depicted in this book are entirely fictitious. Any resemblance to real people or situations is entirely coincidental and unintentional.
– The authors, editors, and publisher

Acknowledgements

We are deeply grateful to Pepperdine University and The Straus Institute and, in particular, to Managing Director Professor Peter Robinson for all of the excellent advice and continuing support of our endeavours as educators in the field of communication and conflict resolution.

We also wish to thank Pepperdine Adjunct Professor and Mediator Jeff Krivis of Los Angeles for the incredible learning opportunities provided to both of us. Mr. Krivis is one of the most experienced mediators in the field in the United States. His insights were invaluable.

We acknowledge that this book could not have been written without permission from Harvard Professors Douglas Stone, Sheila Heen, and Bruce Patton of The Harvard University Negotiation Project and Dr. William Isaacs, Sloan School of Management. We wish to thank them for allowing us to make reference to some of their numerous publications in the field of conflict resolution and communication protocols and their research in the fields of mediation and principled negotiation.

We extend a profound thank you to Brian D. Stewart, M.D., FRCPC, physician leader, Calgary, and Tanis Blench, M.D., M.B.A., both of whom are highly experienced and dedicated physicians. Their insightful review of our materials and their comments helped us focus on the issues of conflict that are of particular interest and relevance to healthcare professionals.

Finally, we would like to acknowledge the support of Alberta Health Services, which was essential in bringing this project to fruition. ∎

Contents

Healthcare professionals show incredible skill and dedication but are not immune to conflict. How does communication breakdown and conflict in workplace interaction affect healthcare professionals and their patients? What is "principled negotiation?" How can acute and chronic conflict in the healthcare environment affect the final outcome of medical care?

What knowledge do healthcare professionals require to make informed choices about conflict resolution processes? What is the five-stage model of negotiation? Can negotiation and mediation help healthcare professionals avoid costly arbitration or litigation?

When is conflict positive? What are the unique dynamics of communication in the healthcare environment? How do the underlying needs of the parties to conflict affect their relationship? What styles of negotiation are most effective in healthcare? What is *your* conflict-handling "style?"

Why is it difficult to think and act in a reasonable manner when conflict arises? How does conflict affect the entire workplace? Why do some conflicts spiral out of control?

Why do the rational and cognitive processes commonly used by physicians in their practices tend to escalate conflict with their colleagues? How does the work environment and organizational culture in healthcare contribute to conflict? Why are certain healthcare workers viewed as disruptive? How can a facilitator to conflict identify the underlying needs of the parties?

The potential for conflict is inherent in the delivery of healthcare. Parties must learn how to take steps to break down the causes of conflict into manageable pieces using the techniques and tools of principled communication.

Foreword

The word "mentor" is a Greek term, originating from Homer's *The Odyssey*. When Odysseus, the king of Ithaca, went off to fight the Trojan War, he entrusted the care of his son, Telemachus, to his friend Mentor, a wise teacher. Thus the word mentor has come to mean a trusted friend, counsellor, or teacher, an experienced guide or coach.

I met Heather Lamoureux and Elaine Seifert when they were second-career students attending the Straus Institute for Dispute Resolution at Pepperdine Law School in Malibu, California. I had the pleasure of serving as a mentor to each of them as they studied effective ways to mediate conflicts. It was an honour to be entrusted with this task.

Before embarking on a career in conflict resolution, both Heather and Elaine were highly successful in their chosen professions: Heather being a long-standing judge and Elaine a well-respected business and family law practitioner in Calgary, Alberta. They, like other professionals who embark on second careers, often sacrifice precious time and financial resources to broaden their impact and make a difference in the world. Many successful people attend the Straus Institute in order to expand their skills in their own fields, but some seek to apply the principles of mediation in new fields and new ways. Heather and Elaine are just such professionals.

In their professional careers, and now with this fine book, they show how breakthroughs in conflict resolution can be made in the critical field of healthcare. Unfortunately, when conflict arises amidst medical endeavours, a patient's health is in jeopardy. Critical decisions are delayed, healthcare practitioners are distracted, and the patient becomes a sidebar to other issues. In applying the many skills and techniques of conflict resolution to healthcare, this book serves as a guide for those heroes in our society—healthcare practitioners—to alleviate distractions and focus their attention on serving the healthcare needs of their community. When such conflict arises, it is critical that the distributors of good healthcare have the tools to manage the conflict so that patients receive the best care they have to offer.

This book provides practical insights into everyday issues that arise in hospitals and in doctors' offices, where the problem that gets in the way of delivering the best healthcare available is often an act of misunderstanding that could easily be solved by better understanding and good communication skills.

In a very real sense, this treatise places Heather and Elaine in the entrusted role of mentors to the healthcare industry as they begin the awesome task of managing conflict so that lives can be saved. ■

Jeffrey Krivis
February 2009
Los Angeles, California

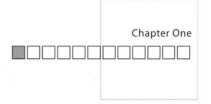

Chapter One

Current Communication Environment in Canadian Hospitals

he dynamics of interaction among professionals in healthcare are often exciting, invigorating, and positive. The marvels of medical teamwork in heart-transplant surgery, the sophistication of multidisciplinary teams in genetic research, and the complex triage processes in place in the emergency room all point to the incredible intelligence, dedication, and training of physicians, nurses, and other members of the healthcare profession.

And yet this amazing, lively dynamic is not infrequently an environment where conflict occurs—interpersonal and unpleasant human interaction with potential negative consequences for healthcare providers and their patients.

Communication breakdown and conflict in workplace interaction not only adversely affects the work environment but its continued unresolved existence contributes to systemic problems that may ultimately compromise patient care. Research suggests that a plethora of issues—centred on communication breakdown—impairs the delivery of efficient, user-friendly healthcare at all levels: the walk-in medical clinic, the physician's office, the resident-training programs, the triage unit in emergency, the operating room, and at bedside in hospitals.[1+2]

Even the simple act of the nurse or physician failing to *actively* listen, to engage in the process of open questioning, to reframe a negative statement in the patient-physician, patient-nurse, nurse-physician interaction can adversely affect the final outcome of medical care.[3] Dr. Jorge Carreras, a faculty member in the Miles Program for Physician-Patient Communication at the Memorial Mission Hospital, Asheville, North Carolina, noted in an article on doctor-patient relationships that: "Once interrupted, patients readily relinquish control over the dialogue to the physician, who, at such an early stage, may not have sufficient information to make an accurate diagnosis or to channel the flow of information from the patients."[4+5]

Good professional behaviour involves the development, nurturing, and maintenance of strong communication skills together with the ability to resolve conflict in a principled process. This principled process is identified and will be referred to throughout this book as "principled negotiation." Principled negotiation can be defined as a collaborative process of engagement in dialogue and interaction that culminates in win-win for all parties to a conflict.

What do we mean by dialogue? How can healthcare professionals engage in dialogue in an efficient, expeditious manner to resolve disputes in an informal setting without resorting to adversarial processes such as litigation and arbitration, which usually result in a clear winner and an unfortunate loser? Adversarial processes, while useful in cases where a crime has been committed or a legal precedent must be created, are usually expensive and time consuming. The development of dialogue through principled negotiation has the capacity to resolve the vast majority of conflict scenarios in the healthcare environment.

The first step toward creation of the win-win in communication and conflict is the recognition that difficult conversations cannot be endlessly avoided. Rather we must learn, practise, and embrace dialogue as a means of engaging in these complex conversations. True dialogue is the antithesis of debate and argument.

While debate and argument are centred on the concept of a winner and a loser, dialogue creates winners all around. Dialogue is the quintessential "win-win" for everyone who chooses to engage.

In the workplace context, dialogue can be defined as "a sustained collective search for shared meaning through verbal exchange."[6] Dialogue does not have an agenda, a leader, a pre-ordained task, or a PowerPoint presentation. Healthcare professionals who engage in dialogue do not seek to solve familiar problems in a familiar way, nor do they focus their inquiry on the past. Dialogue leads to forward thinking and future action.

Dialogue is exploration through conversation:

- Exploration of assumptions controlling our behaviour in the workplace.

- Exploration of the "myths" of long-held conclusions that have governed the rules of behaviour in the workplace.

- Exploration of the action, interaction, and inaction in the interpersonal engagement of professionals.

True dialogue reveals the "big picture" and the communication network: its strengths, weaknesses, gaps, and connections. We urge our readers to read the book *Dialogue and the Art of Thinking Together* by William Isaacs as it is the originating source of ideas summarized in this chapter.[7]

The first step in the process of engaging in dialogue, according to Professor Isaacs, is to learn how to listen to and negotiate with ourselves! We must undertake the initially uncomfortable process of recognizing naïve realism—that bundle of thoughts that often leads us to the incorrect conclusion that we alone know the truth underlying any particular problem or conflict and that it is just a matter of convincing others to accept that truth in order to "fix it." Professor Isaacs cautions us to learn to mistrust our initial inferences and hastily drawn conclusions. Instead, we must begin the process of dialogue by asking ourselves this crucial question: What information might I be missing?

Second, we must recognize and overcome our natural tendency toward negative attribution—the often misleading conclusion that others in the workplace environment must have bad intentions toward us. We must recognize and disregard the nagging inner thought that "they are just out to get me!" Instead, we must learn to begin a conversation with the belief that the other party may be acting with good or at least neutral intentions toward us.

Third, we must seek to quell the inner voice of false self-assurance that drives us to conclude that "everyone else" is to blame for the current problem. Instead, the first question we must learn to ask ourselves is "what might I have done to contribute to this problem?"

Alan Webber, the former editor of *The Harvard Business Review*, theorizes that the most important work in the twenty-first century in this new economy is that of creating conversations, of creating dialogue. All organizations, writes Webber, are nothing more and nothing less than networks of conversations.

> Dialogue can give us a way to regain that gold standard (of meaning). It does this by helping create an atmosphere in which we can perceive what really matters ... doing so gives us access to a much finer and subtler kind of intelligence than we might ordinarily encounter.[8]

The focus of this book is to describe and outline a process for effective communication amongst all players in healthcare—a process designed to resolve acute and chronic conflict in the health services environment.[9] We will outline and explain a simple five-stage model for managing conflict in healthcare called the "Principled Negotiation Model":

Stage 1 – Pre-meeting Preparation

Stage 2 – Convening the Meeting

Stage 3 – Creating the Agenda: Identifying Issues and Interests

Stage 4 – Brainstorming Options for Mutual Gain

Stage 5 – Reaching Agreement: Evaluation and Implementation

Unmet, misunderstood, and conflicting human needs—both phys-ical and psychological—act as a catalyst for both chronic and acute conflict.[10] Readers of this book will learn to master com-munication skills for their own needs and the needs of others in the workplace. They will learn strategies for discussing conflict with co-workers in a reasoned manner and resolving issues with-out resorting to expensive, time-consuming adversarial processes. It is our expectation that readers will learn how to gain control over their professional interactions and their work environment in a manner that preserves peace and promotes the accomplishment of their goals in the workplace. ■

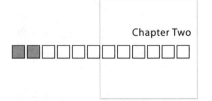

Chapter Two

Conflict Resolution through the Five Stages of Principled Negotiation

When conflict arises it is critical that parties to the conflict understand the various conflict-resolution processes—negotiation, mediation, arbitration, and litigation—to allow them to make informed choices about which process to undertake.

Negotiation is a voluntary process involving direct dialogue between the parties, with no independent third party involved. The process of negotiation is designed by the parties, the exchange of ideas and information is private, and there is no binding adjudication dictating a particular result. The negotiation may be win-lose, win-win, or lose-lose depending on the process of dialogue undertaken. The dialogue may be distributive, where each party tries to gain as much for themselves as possible, or interest based, where each party tries to reach a resolution that will meet the needs of all parties to the negotiation.

Mediation is "a private voluntary dispute-resolution process in which a third party neutral, invited by all the parties, assists the parties in identifying issues of mutual concern, developing options for resolving those issues and finding resolutions acceptable to all parties."[11]

Mediation, like negotiation, is informal and private. The mediator, working with the parties, will assist the parties to design a process for the identification of issues and needs and for the exchange of facts and relevant information. The mediator will assist the parties to identify their win-win options for mutual gain. The process of mediation does not involve adjudication. Although the parties may give the mediator power to evaluate their respective positions, the focus of mediation is to create a win-win for all parties to the conflict.

Arbitration is "a private voluntary dispute resolution process where the parties to a dispute agree in writing to submit the dispute for binding resolution to a third party neutral, chosen by the parties."[12] Parties to an arbitration do have some control over the design of the process and mutually select the neutral to decide their case. Arbitration is private. The decision of the arbitrator is final and binding upon the parties, subject only to limited rights of appeal to a court. The outcome of arbitration, like litigation, is often win-lose.

Litigation is "an involuntary, formal, public process for dispute resolution, where a judge and/or jury determine facts, decrees and outcome to legal causes of action based on adversarial presentations by each party."[13] Litigation creates binding results and public precedents. The adversarial nature of the process, which is dictated by statute law, common law, and rules of court, does not promote collaboration or cooperation. Litigation is limited to resolution of issues that can be translated into legal causes of action. Litigation usually requires the parties to retain expert legal representation.

The vast majority of conflict scenarios encountered in healthcare do not require resort to arbitration, hearings before tribunals, or litigation in order to resolve successfully. The majority of parties to a dispute, once familiar with the practices and procedures outlined in this book, should be able to resolve their conflicts on their own without requiring expensive and time-consuming formal processes such as litigation or arbitration.

The focus of this chapter is to outline the five steps of principled negotiation that can be used successfully by the parties themselves to resolve conflict. The model is user friendly, inexpensive, and expeditious. It was originally developed and explained by Harvard Professors Roger Fisher, William Ury, and Bruce Patton in the best-selling book *Getting to Yes*.[14] This chapter outlines and expands upon the steps originally expressed in *Getting to Yes*.

Step 1 – Pre-meeting Preparation

Most parties to conflict prepare before meeting. Gathering facts, preparing PowerPoint presentations and reports, engaging experts, and outlining positions are all almost routine tasks undertaken before a meeting commences. However, we use the word "preparation" in a somewhat different context. Parties who seek conflict resolution, whether in negotiation or mediation, should prepare to answer the following questions *before* the meeting commences:

1. What is my position? (What solution do I want?)

2. What do I think the other parties' position might be? (Their solution to the conflict.)

3. How can I frame the positions in neutrally worded issues acceptable to both parties?

4. What needs (physical, safety, social, self-esteem, attainment of professional goals in the workplace) might underlie my position in the conflict?

5. Can I "hunch" what the other parties' needs in the conflict might be?[15]

6. What is my best alternative to a negotiated agreement (my BATNA)? In short, is there a better outcome than what is being offered in the negotiation?[16]

7. Can I hunch what the opposing parties' BATNA might be?

Let us look at an example to see how this type of preparation might work in a potential conflict between an employee and employer.

> Dr. Bones was hired to head ABC Hospital's Emergency Department. She moved to Canada from the United States, with a promise of salary commensurate to her experience and equal to those of department heads at other Canadian hospitals. After six months on the job (on a three-year contract), Dr. Bones has discovered that she may be receiving $85,000 less in annual salary than other emergency department heads at similar hospitals. She is furious and has requested a meeting with hospital administration.

Here is what Dr. Bones's private preparation notes might look like in our hypothetical scenario.

1. What is my position? I want the same salary as other department heads of emergency departments.

2. [Hunch] What is the other party's position? Perhaps the hospital is paying what the budget allows; they see my department responsibilities as less onerous than other department heads, hence less salary to me.

3. What neutral words can I use to express an issue we can jointly discuss? Perhaps "fair compensation for Dr. Bones" as department head.

4. What are my needs?

   • economic

   • self-esteem—to be paid the same as my peers

   • fair recognition for education and experience

5. What are the hospital's needs?

   • economic?

6. What is my BATNA? What reasonable course of action could I take in the absence of agreement in order to achieve my needs? Perhaps begin a search for other employment while continuing to work under the current contract.

7. What is best hunch of hospital administration's BATNA? Stand firm—"a deal is a deal"—do nothing and let Dr. Bones take the first step.

The foregoing process of preparation serves a number of useful purposes:

1. Preparation will require parties to reality check the potential outcomes if no settlement is agreed upon.

2. Preparation initiates the process of moving from positions: i.e., "I want ..." to framing of issues, i.e., "We need to talk about ... Issue 1, Issue 2, Issue 3."

3. Preparation allows the parties to examine the complexity of the conflict and the number of issues that must be addressed. This, in turn, may lead to an informed decision to bring in a mediator to assist in the process.

No conflict can ever be resolved from a mere statement of the parties' positions. This crucial first step of preparation greatly increases the opportunity for resolution.

Step 2 – Convening the Meeting

In this state of conflict resolution, parties must actively consider *who* will come to the meeting, *where* they will meet, *when* they will meet, *how* the meeting will be structured, and *what* ground rules will govern attendees' behaviour at the meeting.

In summary:

- Who?
- Where?
- When?
- How?
- What?

These are the five crucial questions that must be addressed before dialogue on the conflict can be initiated. Mediators call this stage "the convening stage." In healthcare terms it is akin to the protocols that must be established and followed in the laboratory in order to achieve an explainable, defendable outcome.

Who must be at the meeting?

It is important to have decision makers and the parties with the requisite level of authority to make the agreement that is to be implemented. It is a waste of time and effort for parties to attend a five-hour meeting only to have one party indicate that they do not have authority to "sign off" and that they must go through the process of convincing someone else (not at the meeting) before the agreement can be implemented.

Where should the meeting occur?

Most parties to conflict give little thought to the location for a meeting, yet the choice of location can exert a powerful influence on the mood of the parties in attendance. Meetings that occur in hot, windowless, cluttered rooms are often fraught with irritated, hurried exchanges by individuals anxious to conclude and get out of the room!

It is important that parties to a conflict address their meeting's physical environment: room size, chair and table set-up, and physical amenities (food, water, light). Will there be a round table with comfortable chairs or will the table reflect a hierarchy with a long rectangular board-room type table with a head and an end? Will the meeting occur at the office of the party perceived to be the most powerful or will the parties meet at a neutral location? Location sets the tone. Room set-up creates the ambiance. Parties must consciously address these issues to create a psychological incentive to resolve the conflict.

When will the meeting happen?

Timing is everything in life and no less so in the workplace. Who sets the time for a meeting to discuss a conflict can often create a subtle reality of control, exerting control over when the meeting begins, when breaks will occur (if at all), and when parties will adjourn.

If collaborative dialogue is to occur, the question of timing must be addressed in a collaborative manner. The party who requires an 8:00 A.M. start, who does not want breaks, who insists on a predetermined end time, etc., has already adversely affected the parties' potential for principled dialogue and win-win resolution of the conflict. Timing must be a mutual decision discussed openly and agreed upon by everyone who needs to be in the room.

How will the meeting be structured?

The structure of the meeting creates the perception of fairness, which is a powerful catalyst for agreement. Will each party have an equal opportunity to outline their view of the conflict? Will the meeting involve personal attendances or will some attend via video conference? Will the meeting occur in one location or several locations? Will the meeting be recorded in some fashion? What technical or expert assistance—PowerPoint presentations, white board, laser printers, DVDs, oral presentations, written material—will be most effective to delineate the issues and discern the underlying needs of the parties? Is it necessary to have a chair-person? What confidentiality agreements, if any, will be required to protect the statements made at the meeting? Generally, confi-dentiality agreements state that all discussions are confidential and that none of the information disclosed in the meeting will be dis-cussed nor will any of the disclosure made in the meeting be dis-seminated outside the meeting. What disclosure of any agreements made will be required? Disclosure required will depend on the matters or issues being discussed but generally refers to all docu-ments and information that are relevant to the matters being dis-cussed and that the parties can agree to disclose. This disclosure of course will be subject to the confidentiality provisions.[17]

What will be the ground rules at the meeting?

The ground rules for the interaction must be the subject of dis-cussion and collaborative agreement *before* dialogue on the posi-tions and issues can occur. Conflict resolution is a group endeavour. The group must decide on the ground rules and what will happen if someone is not following the rules. Who speaks first? Will receiving calls, texting, taking cell phone messages be allowed? What about interruption during speech? Will parties have an opportunity to state their view of the history of the con-flict uninterrupted? Will yelling be tolerated? Profanity? Making faces? Pen or pencil tapping? Whispering to someone while an-other party is speaking? Is this endured or prohibited?

All of these questions are essential. Parties to conflict would be well advised to address them together in a conscientious manner in a preliminary planning meeting in order to build a solid plat-form for dialogue and resolution.

In our experience meetings are most effective when parties are physically present and are able to determine the structure of the meeting together. It is also important that ample time be pro-vided for each party to be able to outline their concerns and equally participate in any ensuing discussions. The use of DVD, PowerPoint, and other visual aids at these meetings are generally best left to matters or issues that may be complicated and require extensive explanation.

Step 3 – Creating the Agenda: Identifying Issues and Interests

In Chapter Nine, we will explore the process of changing positions into issues and the subsequent probing of issues to determine the needs and interests of the parties. We will discuss the necessity of determining the common underlying needs and interests of the parties.

Chapter Nine also reviews the process of creating the collaborative agenda. The aim of agenda creating is to create a list of neutrally worded statements that will enable all parties to agree to meet to discuss them. This step is crucial to the success of principled communication and conflict resolution as it defuses non-productive emotional thought and allows parties to begin to see the conflict as a series of common issues that can be worked on in a collaborative manner as a team. The neutrally worded agenda breaks the tension and allows parties to begin to focus on underlying needs and interests.

Step 4 – Brainstorming Options for Mutual Gain

In Chapter Ten we will review five elements to successful brainstorming of potential solutions to conflict:

1. Assume that we have only partial knowledge (and by inference that others may have the knowledge we lack).

2. Grant legitimacy to the other perspectives in the dialogue.

3. Assume positive intentions on the part of others.

4. Acknowledge that our words and actions might have unin-

tentional consequences—be open to learning and understanding how others are affected by our proposed solutions to conflict.

5. Embrace learning.

Brainstorming requires a change to our thinking habits engendered by curiosity.

Step 5 – Reaching Agreement: Evaluation and Implementation

In Chapter Eleven we will review the final step in the Principled Negotiation Model. Below, we have outlined the four questions that must be asked by parties as they evaluate the efficacy of potential solutions:

1. Is it feasible?

2. Does it address the parties' common interests?

3. Is it fair? Does it meet objective criteria?

4. Can it be implemented?

We will also discuss the use of objective criteria and outline the elements of planning for implementation of solutions. ■

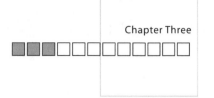

Chapter Three

Needs and
Personalities

I t is reasonably certain in the below scenario that when Dr. Doe has his first communication with the junior resident in emergency there will be conflict.

> Dr. John Doe, a senior cardiology resident, is inwardly seething as he walks down the grey-green corridor of the hospital toward the triage area. It is 5:00 A.M. A junior resident had called him earlier for an urgent consultation on a patient admitted an hour ago for unremitting chest pain.[18]
>
> "Why don't they train these guys the way I was trained? How come I have to hold their hands? I certainly didn't go to medical school and specialty training for nine years to be called at 5:00 A.M. by some junior resident who hasn't taken the time to properly assess the patient!" he thinks to himself as he slams open the door to emergency and strides over to the unit nurse.

Conflict is a natural product of the dynamics of intersecting needs in the workplace. In many senses, conflict can be viewed as positive. It may work as a catalyst toward a positive change in behaviour. Unfortunately, a great deal of conflict that occurs in the work environment leads to negative interactions affecting the development of positive working relationships. Author Thomas Crum, in his book *The Magic of Conflict,* wrote: "It is not whether you have conflict in your life. It is what you do with that conflict that makes a difference."[19]

In order to analyze the cause of conflict and to develop protocols for turning negative interactions into a positive force, health professionals must understand the unique dynamics of communication in the healthcare environment.

Communication most simply explained is the sending and receiving of messages: verbal, written, or non-verbal. Defleur, Osgood, Schramm, and Dance[20] developed a model for communication suggesting that interpretation of messages being transmitted from one party to another is in fact circular, dynamic, and inextricably interconnected (circular model) to the relationship between the parties. Jessica Galante[21], along with other researchers in the field of communication, have theorized that ultimately the meaning of the message and the interpretation of the conflict may be different for the sender and the receiver. The circular model suggests that the underlying causes of the conflict may be driven by the underlying needs of the parties and their past experiences and relationships.

The underlying needs of each party to a communication in the workplace may further be viewed from five perspectives:

1. The physical needs (proper work schedules, adequate space, tools, light, breaks, a degree of privacy in which the communication occurs).

2. The safety of that environment from the perspective of the perceived freedom of the parties to communicate.

3. The social context of the communication from the perspective of formal and informal opportunities given to the parties to interact, including the protocols established in the environment, as well as the degree to which the organization encourages a sense of belonging, with respect to verbal and written communication.

4. The ego needs of the parties: the extent to which the communication is affected by their perception that the overall environment nurtures self-esteem, a sense of value in the workplace, and a sense of core principles that satisfy and promote the advancement and status of the individual worker.

5. Self-fulfillment needs: the ultimate success of the communication will be affected by the often unstated sense of empowerment and creativity that the parties have in the workplace and whether the workplace allows them to realize their personal goals for achievement as individuals.

The concept of underlying needs acting as a significant factor in conflict was best described and developed in studies undertaken by Maslow in "A Theory of Human Motivation." Maslow stated in his summary of these needs:

> There are at least five sets of goals, which we may call basic needs. They are briefly: physiological, safety, love (social), esteem, and self-actualization. In addition, we are motivated by the desire to achieve or maintain the various conditions upon which these basic satisfactions rest and certain more intellectual desires. These basic goals are related to each other, being arranged in a hierarchy of prepotency...[W]hen a need is fairly well satisfied, the next preponent (higher) need emerges in turn to dominate the conscious life and to serve as the center of organization of behaviour, since gratified needs are not active motivators.[22]

A schematic illustration of Maslow's Hierarchy of Needs can be found below.

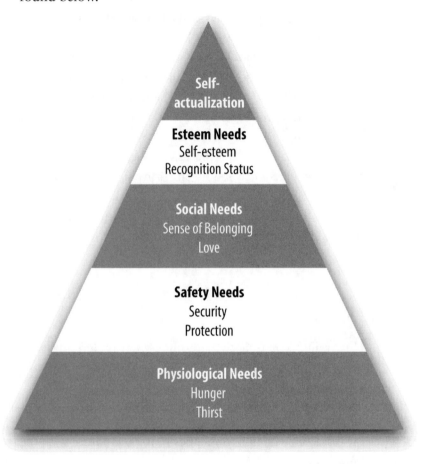

Maslow's Hierarchy of Needs is of direct relevance to the current analysis of conflict in the medical environment.

From the perspective of underlying needs, let us now examine the exchange that is going to occur between Dr. Doe and the junior resident, Dr. Saline, who has called for the consult in our fictitious scenario.

As Dr. Doe enters the triage room, Dr. Saline, the junior resident doing his emergency rotation, approaches him. Before Dr. Saline can speak, Dr. Doe says in an irritated voice: "What is your problem, Dr. Saline? Why am I being called at 5:00 A.M. to deal with this matter that could easily be handled once the patient is admitted to CCU?"

Dr. Saline replies, "Dr. Doe, I had no choice. I can't stabilize this patient. I need your help."

"Fine, Dr. Saline," Dr. Doe replies sarcastically. "I always seem to be called when you are on call in emergency. I'll see the patient, but you are going to have to learn to make clinical decisions by yourself without feeling the need to check with me all the time!"

Imagine now that you, the reader, are the junior resident confronted with the angry senior resident.

- How might you quickly determine what underlying need or needs may be driving the sarcastic response of Dr. Doe, according to Maslow's Hierarchy of Needs?

- What communication could be quickly directed to the senior resident to instil in him a desire to collaborate with the junior resident?

- In this scenario, negative emotions are driving the communication. The senior resident is frustrated and impatient. Will it help to ask why? Will it change the dynamics of the communication to advise the senior resident that the junior resident will not engage until he "calms down?" Can the conflict be "cured" by reporting the senior resident's behaviour to the program director? Will that make it worse? How might you respond if the senior resident elevates the conflict through profanity or engages in intimidating behaviour or threatens to report you to the program director?

These are all relevant questions to ask and consider. The answers will be forthcoming as we outline a communication process that adopts a collaborative conflict-resolution style. This approach to communication and conflict resolution is routinely referred to in the literature as *principled* communication.

In subsequent chapters we will analyze this interaction from the perspective of needs and differing conflict-handling behaviours of healthcare professionals. We will present techniques for uncovering these underlying needs to assist readers to understand how to de-escalate conflict and move it toward brainstorming options for mutual gain in a collaborative manner. We will talk about *changing* the dynamic of this fictitious conflict through the processes of active listening, clarifying, paraphrasing, summarizing, open-ended questioning, reframing, as well as changing blame to needs, judgments to questions, and positions to interests.

Utilizing this analysis, the following dialogue could occur between the junior resident and the senior resident.

Dr. Doe (rushing into emergency), out of breath, face flushed and irritated: "Why have you called for a consult at 5:00 A.M. on this patient? Can you not care for this patient until my rounds start at 7:00 A.M.?"

Dr. Saline: "I know you are tired, and I am sorry to have to call you at this early hour. However—"

Dr. Doe: "But this is simple stuff! You just don't trust your own clinical judgment. You know it is unstable angina ..."

Dr. Saline: "You may be right that I should have known this, but I feel that I am unable to stabilize the patient sufficiently to risk transferring him to CCU. I am sorry that I had to call you for a consult so early in the morning."

In this dialogue we can observe the junior resident perceiving and immediately addressing the underlying need of the senior resident—related to ego—for status recognition, appreciation, and respect. We can also notice the successful defusing of potential conflict by the junior resident when he acknowledges that the senior resident may be right to be irritated and upset. The acknowledgement, if properly given, may encourage the senior resident's inclination to collaborate with the junior resident. The junior resident agrees that:

- The senior resident is probably fatigued.

- It is early in the morning.

- The junior resident *may* be lacking in confidence and clinical experience in devising a treatment protocol for unstable angina.

All of the potential points for argument are met head-on and their validity has been acknowledged. The ego needs of the senior resident have also been addressed. There may now be a higher likelihood of collaboration in the future, although it will probably be necessary for the junior resident to address the question of whether the senior resident's conduct is exhibited toward other members of the healthcare team. If so, there may be a chronic conflict that will require a meeting with the senior resident to address the long-term issue of professional behaviour. In Chapter Six we will review the communication tools necessary to facilitate such a meeting.

The Relationship between Conflict-handling Style and Communication Skills during Conflict

The capacity to handle communication effectively and to solve workplace conflict is further affected by the innate conflict-handling behaviour of the individual participants. It would be unrealistic to develop a principled conflict resolution without recognizing the realities of emotion and different styles of handling conflict of the players involved in conflict. This is true for the healthcare profession as it is for any organization that seeks to implement conflict-resolving processes. In the real world, emotions are always present either overtly or under the surface. Further, various conflict-handling styles are present in any organization. Strategies that work with the competitive people (assertive and uncooperative) may fail with the passive individuals (unassertive and uncooperative). The effective resolution of conflict in a principled manner will in part depend upon identification of the conflict-handling behaviour of the professionals as well as discerning their underlying needs.

Ken Thomas and Ralph Kilmann[23] identified various learned behaviours for dealing with conflict in the context of negotiation styles. Thomas and Kilmann co-authored *The Thomas-Kilmann Conflict Mode Instrument,* which allowed participants to test and define five conflict-handling styles that are influenced by the behavioral dimensions individuals experience in conflict. These behavioral dimensions are the level of assertiveness or the extent to which an individual attempts to satisfy his own needs and the level of cooperativeness or the extent to which an individual works toward satisfying needs of the other party.

A. The **competitor** negotiation style was identified as highly assertive and minimally cooperative. This individual seeks to win and is comfortable in win-lose scenarios and has few collaborative skills. The competitor is essentially concerned with dictating a decision. Typically a competitor will take a position in the bargaining or negotiation and will indicate that the only solution is the "my way" solution. The competitor is a hard bargainer who will strive to protect his or her own interests from attack.

B. At the other end of the spectrum is the **collaborator**, who will seek to work with other parties to the conflict in an effort to arrive at a solution that satisfies the interests of all the parties to the conflict. The collaborator emphasizes the potential for conflict resolution in a win-win approach. The collaborator is constantly looking at the conflict from the perspective of determining solutions that allow all parties to feel heard, understood, and involved in the resolution process. The collaborator values strong relationships and innovative solutions to conflict that address the underlying needs of the parties. The collaborator is highly cooperative and highly assertive.

C. Between the diametrically opposed behavioural dimensions of competitor and collaborator, there are other conflict-handling behaviours with different approaches to the resolution of conflict. The **avoider** often refuses to deal overtly with conflict. The avoider is uncomfortable with conflict and will seek to avoid stress by minimizing contact with unpleasant people or situations. The avoider essentially seeks to steer clear of conflict in the hope that it will disappear, dissipate, or be resolved by someone else. The avoider is uncooperative and unassertive.

D. The accommodating conflict-handling behaviour describes the individual who seeks to meet the needs of others in priority to his or her own needs. The **accommodator** seeks to resolve conflict by addressing the underlying needs and issues of other parties in the hope and expectation that by doing so the conflict will disappear. The accommodator values harmony and will often choose a quick ending or an easy solution to the conflict. The accommodator is highly cooperative and minimally assertive.

E. Finally, we have the **compromiser**. The compromiser is not necessarily interested in delving deeply into the interests of either party in a conflict. He or she simply wants an expedient, efficient solution. The compromiser will always seek to provide equal gains and equal losses to resolve the conflict by each party simply cutting their losses and giving up whatever it takes in order to achieve resolution. The compromiser is neither overly assertive nor overly cooperative.

It is possible to utilize one, some, or all of the various conflict-handling styles during conflict. Ken Thomas in his article "What Is the Best Way to Handle Conflict?" outlines the benefits and disadvantages of each behaviour.[24] For example, the competitor may achieve a quick decision. The compromiser may reduce the strain on working relationships by meeting co-workers halfway. The avoider may gain time to become better prepared. The accommodator may achieve social capital by helping and apologizing when necessary. However, the collaborator, according to Thomas, is the individual capable of achieving the highest quality decisions. It is the collaborator who is capable of uncovering "principled" solutions to conflict that work on a long-term basis to change communication patterns for the entire working environment.

It is also possible for individuals to move between conflict-handling styles or modify their conflict-handling style depending on a number of variables such as the situation and context of the interaction, the importance of the issue being negotiated, the importance of the relationship between the parties to the conflict, and the conflict-handling style of the other party.

Talking Points

i) Conflict is driven by interference in basic human needs as identified by A.H. Maslow. In order to resolve conflict successfully it is important to be aware of those needs in yourself and others.

ii) Conflict is also either driven or resolved by conflict-handling styles of those involved in the interaction. Recognition of your own conflict-handling style and that of the other parties to the conflict is essential in the successful application of a principled approach to conflict resolution.

iii) In order to analyze the cause of conflict and to develop protocols for turning negative interactions into a positive force, healthcare professionals must understand the unique dynamics of communication in the healthcare environment.

iv) Healthcare personnel are intuitive, and intuition works to assist them with the provision of care. Having a sense of the conflict-management style of individuals involved in a conflict scenario will assist the individual healthcare workers in determining a strategy/process for resolving conflict or disagreements that has the greatest likelihood of not only reaching a mutually satisfactory resolution but also maintaining the relationship between the parties. ■

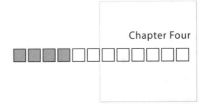

Chapter Four

Conflict Escalation
and Prevailing Climate in
the Healthcare Environment

lthough conflict usually emerges as a result of the inherent differences between parties or perceived incompatible goals between parties, it does not intensify for these reasons alone. Escalation or an increase in intensity of a conflict results from the actions that the parties take in responding to those differences or incompatibilities. More specifically, the actions and reactions made by the parties create and define the conflict and sustain it.

Conflict theorists Dean Pruitt, Jeffery Rubin, and Sung Hee Kim, in *Social Conflict: Escalation, Stalemate and Settlement,* suggest that as conflict escalates "the parties to the conflict go through incremental transformations" and that "the conflict intensifies in ways that make it difficult to undo."[25] Pruitt, Rubin, and Kim identified five transformations that commonly occur during escalation.[26] First the parties move from light to heavy tactics. Light tactics include "persuasive argument, promises, and attempts to ingrate self with other," while heavy tactics include "threats and irrevocable commitments." Next the conflict grows in size. As conflict intensifies there is a tendency for issues to proliferate and more resources to be committed to the struggle. "Specific issues then tend to give way to general issues and the overall relationship between the parties starts to deteriorate."[27] Participants tend to grow from a few to many as the parties recruit others to their cause. Finally, the parties' objectives change from doing well to outdoing the other and then hurting the other. Pruitt, Rubin, and Kim further suggest that every action or re-action of one party becomes suspect to the other party, who responds in terms of how they have interpreted the action or reaction. Unfor-tunately, once people are in conflict they become increasingly suspi-cious of each other, rigid in how they see the problem and limited in recognizing solutions that may be available to address the issues. As conflict intensifies, all kinds of consequences spiral outward, affect-ing individuals, relationships, tasks, decisions, and gradually spread-ing to a point where it involves the whole group or organization.[28]

Dr. Jane Doe is a junior physician in the oncology division at a major hospital. The work environment is very tense, and often there is disagreement among the doctors on how to run the department, on patient treatment, the call schedule, and educational opportunities. The divisional head, Dr. Blood, is intent on running the department the way it has always been run and is not receptive to input from other doctors in the department, especially the more junior doctors and residents.

Dr. Doe is finding it very difficult to continue to work in this division. She is always stressed and afraid to make suggestions for improvement. She recently made what she thought was an excellent suggestion at a staff meet-ing regarding procedure in their division. Dr. Blood was obviously irate with her for making this suggestion and dismissed it without discussion. Dr. Doe has made other comments during her rounds about patients' diagnoses or treatment, and again Dr. Blood dismissed her com-ments without discussion. Dr. Doe has talked to the other junior doctors. They feel the same way she does but think that maybe Dr. Blood is harder on her than on the others. They have suggested to her that perhaps she asks too many questions, and that it is better to just go along with Dr. Blood than try to change things.

Dr. Blood is suspicious of Dr. Doe. She is always trying to change things and implying that his methods are outdated. He feels that she tries to embarrass him at meetings. He has been at this a long time and maybe he is not as familiar with all the new medications, etc., but he knows what he is doing and doesn't want to be challenged by this young doctor. He finds her very difficult to talk to so tries to avoid her if he can. He has discussed her behaviour with his friend in the division, Dr. Bones, who also finds her a bit confrontational.

There is constant tension and unease between Dr. Doe and Dr. Blood, and things are reaching a boiling point. The new call schedule has come out, and Dr. Doe thinks it is totally unfair. She believes that Dr. Blood has set the schedule to favour himself and his friend Dr. Bones and to interfere with her summer plans as retaliation for challenging him at the meeting. She calls her department head and advises her that she will leave the division unless someone can do something about Dr. Blood.

The above is a typical conflict scenario. A problem emerges, sides are formed, and positions taken. Once positions are taken communication diminishes. As the conflict intensifies, as in the previously described scenario, we often see one or more parties either employing stronger tactics, such as the use of threats, or alternatively withdrawing or avoiding. They become unable to focus on the real issues between them and instead focus on the other party and defeating that party. They become unable to work together to resolve the conflict and a sense of crisis emerges.

Conflict Spiral Illustration[29]

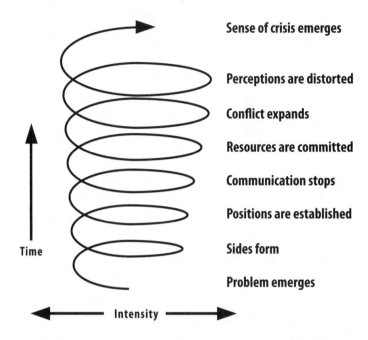

An escalation of conflict is occurring between Dr. Blood and Dr. Doe. Each has taken a position, and communication is seriously impaired. They are making assumptions about the other's behaviour. Every action of Dr. Doe's is interpreted by Dr. Blood as being confrontational, and he reacts to the same by dismissing Dr. Doe or alternatively ignoring her. Dr. Doe in turn suspects that Dr. Blood is intentionally trying to make life difficult for her. Because each is suspicious of the other, each will react to the other with non-collaborative and at times unprofessional tactics that will further instil mistrust and escalate their communication difficulties. They are now unable to work together to resolve this conflict, and others are being brought into the scenario. Without intervention or assistance from a third party, such as a mediator or facilitator, this conflict will continue to spiral, possibly affecting others in the department.

It is important that healthcare professionals are familiar with the effect of "climate" on conflict. Climate can be defined as "the prevailing temper, attitude and outlook of a dyad, group, or organization."[30] It is sometimes referred to as the environment or atmosphere in which interaction takes place. Climate plays an integral role in conflict escalation or resolution because people use their sense of climate to gauge the appropriateness, effectiveness, or likely consequences of their behaviour.

Jack Gibb, in his article "Defensive Communication,"[31] contrasts two types of climates: defensive (tense and evaluative) or supportive (open and non-evaluative). He describes them as below.

Defensive climates are ones where the power is generally invested in one party, there is a lack of trust between the parties, and there is a zero sum mentality in the group (one person's gain has to be another person's loss). In such environments, people make the assumption that the others will act in an aggressive and self-serving way, and thus they adjust their behaviour accordingly. Defensive climates tend to foster uncertainty about how to act and what the consequences of the actions will be. In such climates people come into interactions suspicious and often become focused on protecting themselves. This tends to create similarly defensive reactions in others and prevents the parties from actively engaging in any meaningful communication or problem solving. In defensive climates people tend to react by becoming rigid and defensive. As the parties become more defensive they become less able to accurately perceive motives, values, and emotions underlying the communication. This results in more aggressive use of tactics or, alternatively, avoidance—neither of which is conducive to resolving conflicts.

Supportive or cooperative/non-evaluative climates are ones where power is shared by the group, there is a high degree of trust by the group members, and there is a win-win mentality (the parties can gain by cooperating). Such climates allow people to assess the situation accurately, react in an appropriate manner, and communicate effectively. This tends to produce accurate communication and reinforce supportive behaviour in others. Communication is characterized by descriptive language that encourages discussion and is more oriented to problem solving. Speech is neutral, empathetic (acknowledging the legitimacy of others' emotions), spontaneous, and suggests equality.

Where there is a climate of trust and respect, people will come into an interaction with more open communication and will employ a problem-solving manner to deal with conflict. Conflict has its best chance to move in a productive direction in a supportive climate.

Folger et al suggest the following three measures for changing a climate from defensive to supportive:

1. Undertake small changes in interaction that can eventually result in major changes in climate.

2. Openly discuss themes that trouble the parties. Climate's ability to affect interactions is usually a result of the party's inability to recognize it. If brought out into the open, the parties can consciously move to counteract climate and use it to channel conflict interaction into constructive directions.

3. Intentionally create a critical incident that has the ability to shift the entire direction of the climate.[32]

Returning to the above scenario, the oncology division in which Dr. Doe and Dr. Blood work is a defensive climate. Neither Dr. Blood nor Dr. Doe is sure how to approach the other. They are both mistrustful of the other and therefore have both decided to avoid any interaction with the other party. They are moving into a classic conflict spiral or escalation. Dr. Doe is recruiting other young doctors to her cause. Dr. Blood is recruiting the more senior doctors to his cause. Given their mistrust, inability to communicate, and their recruiting of others to their respective sides, the likelihood of them being able to resolve their issues without the assistance of a facilitator or mediator trained in principled communication is low. It is our experience and recommendation that a facilitator or mediator should be engaged whenever parties have concluded two meetings without resolution of the conflict. Mediators or facilitators should be retained before the parties' respective positions become entrenched and the workplace climate becomes irrevocably defensive. Mediators and trained facilitators possess the requisite skills and knowledge to assist parties in complex, chronic conflict scenarios and can diffuse the escalation of conflict. Parties can then recover a sense of optimism, which will allow them to look forward to conflict resolution.

Fortunately, in the above scenario, Dr. Doe's department head has a background in conflict resolution. By creating a supportive environment for discussion of the issues and employing a principled approach she will be able to encourage Dr. Doe and Dr. Blood to openly discuss the matters that are concerning them. Through the use of effective communication skills, which will be reviewed in Chapter Six, the parties will be able, with the assistance of the department head, to view the problem from the other's perspective and create a shared understanding of each other's needs and interests. They will then be able to problem-solve and come to a resolution that allows them to move forward in the same direction. This change in how the two doctors interact may pave the way for a more open and supportive climate in their work environment, which in turn may help them, and the department as a whole, avoid future conflict-escalation cycles. Changes in chronic defensive climates usually require assistance from a trained facilitator or mediator. The key is for the professional in a defensive climate to recognize the problem early on and seek a strategy (maybe through the assistance of a trained facilitator or mediator) to change the defensive climate.

Talking Points

i) As conflict intensifies, all kinds of consequences spiral out-ward, affecting individuals, relationships, tasks, decisions, and gradually involving the whole group or organization.

ii) There are two types of workplace "climates" in organizations: defensive (tense and evaluative) or supportive (open and non-evaluative):

- Climate's ability to affect interactions is usually a result of the party's inability to recognize it. If brought out into the open, the parties can consciously move to counteract climate and use it to channel conflict into constructive directions.

- Small, cumulative changes in interaction can eventually result in major changes in climate.

iii) Conflict has its best chance to be successfully resolved in a supportive climate.

- Parties to escalating conflict who have endeavoured to resolve it without success would be well advised to retain the services of a facilitator or mediator early on, before their positions become entrenched. ■

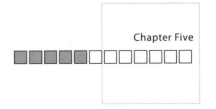

Chapter Five

Procedures and Processes
for Conflict Resolution:
Finding Shared Meaning

r. Jerome Groopman holds the Dina and Raphael Recent Chair of Medicine at Harvard Medical School. Dr. Groopman is the author of the bestseller *How Doctors Think*.[33] He analyzes in astonishing detail the cognitive processes of physicians as they seek to diagnose and treat the twenty-first-century patient. Most physicians, according to Dr. Groopman, invoke expected utility theory,[34] a logical, rational process that is applied across all manner of medical reasoning, even in the face of the manifest uncertainty of modern medicine. This, says Groopman, "... is the core reality of the practice of medicine, where—in the absence of certitude—decisions must be made."[35]

Unfortunately, attempts to use logic and rational processes of expected utility theory as a tool to resolve conflict *within* the medical profession are often fraught with failure. The application of rational, credible, widely practised cognitive processes utilized by physicians and nurses in the diagnosis and treatment of patients and the creation of protocols for resolution of conflict may simply add to and perpetuate problems of negative communication. Why is this? Why do rational discussions, lengthy meetings, carefully planned agendas,

PowerPoint presentations, adjudicated hearings, and evaluative interventions often fail to resolve a conflict? Often such failures occur because these seemingly rational processes fail to identify and address the underlying interests and needs of the parties to the conflict. In failing to identify and address needs, the conflict continues.

In this chapter, we begin to examine the process of conflict resolution based on the discovery of underlying needs. To begin the analysis we present a fictitious meeting of hospital administrators, attending physicians, and senior nurse clinicians.

"The agenda for today's meeting is on the table," says Dr. Steth, the chief hospital administrator. "Please pick up a copy as you enter the meeting room." Everyone sighs, including Dr. Saline.

"Another day, another fruitless meeting. Time will be wasted; nothing will come of it. The decision will be made from the top anyway. So why do they patronize us with these agendas?" thinks Dr. Saline to himself.

1. Minutes from last meeting, review and approval.

2. Controlling disruptive behaviour in interactions. Residents—nursing staff—report from Study Group A.

3. Pending institutional protocols for physician conduct in ER—report from Study Group B.

4. Questions.

"Oh great," Dr. Saline thinks to himself, "another 'done deal' from the study groups. No one ever asked me what the real problems were, and I am certain that the nurses in triage weren't surveyed either. Despite being on the frontline, no one is going to give us any real power to implement change! I'll just tune out and hope my pager goes off so that I have an opportunity to escape as soon as possible."

Many meetings begin with a pre-planned agenda and continue with "reports" from various committees, sub-committees, and study groups, all aimed at fixing the "problem" and removing the conflict. Many of the processes created in the health sector for resolution of conflict, improving communication, or addressing unprofessional behaviour are adjudicative, hierarchical, and judgmental. They seek to label the offending behaviour and to eradicate it.

The Ontario Disruptive Physicians Behaviour Initiative has published an admirable working group report on all aspects of what it defines as "disruptive" behaviour, including a three-stage intervention approach for the management of all aspects of physician behaviour.[36] To its credit, the report addresses the organizational culture and work environment as a potential contributor to frustration, anxiety, and conflict in the health profession. However, the report does not fully examine communication skills aimed at preventing such behaviour in the first instance. The pivotal recommendations of the report address "top down" staged interventions, development of a mandatory code of professionalism in medical schools, implementation of a code of conduct for hospitals with creation of a central authority to receive reports of "problematic behaviour," and a form of "whistle blower" protection for those who do step forward to report such behaviour.

While these are worthwhile initiatives, the report does not address *why* certain healthcare professionals are viewed as "disruptive." Will such processes as those outlined in the Disruptive Physicians Behaviour Initiative quell the problem of physicians who lose their temper, blame others for their problems, or fail to interact in a positive manner with nursing staff, patients, and patients' families? Will agendas, meetings, and committee recommendations address the underlying causes of conflict in the hospital? We are concerned that these initiatives may fall short in creating a permanent positive change in healthcare professional communication. We believe that the issue of healthcare professional behaviour is a small part of a larger metaproblem: the extent to which dialogue and principled communication—leading to positive building of shared goals and innovative solutions—is disappearing from the landscape of verbal, written, and technological exchanges between physicians, between nurses, between physicians and nurses, and between physicians, nurses, and patients.

Some hospitals and medical clinics have working environments analogous to war zones, with factions of healthcare professionals at loggerheads with administration and angry patients waiting in the no man's land of the emergency waiting room. Large sums of money and hours of time have been invested in the creation of new rules and protocols. Patient discontentment, negative communications, and conflict amongst all players in the healthcare system remain unabated and seemingly insoluble. Why is this? The answer may lie in the failure to examine conflict from a principled perspective and to engage all stakeholders in true dialogue to probe their needs.

Doctor William N. Isaacs, the director of the Dialogue Project at MIT's Organizational Learning Center at the Sloan School of Management, has investigated and analyzed this question in a series of articles and books on communication and problem solving in complex organizations including hospitals and HMOs.[37] It is Dr. Isaacs's research that has given rise to the startling hypothesis that there may be no real dialogue, no addressing of underlying interests, and no principled communication in a collective sense occurring in many complex organizations.

In his article "Taking Flight—Dialogue, Collective Thinking and Organizational Learning," Dr. Isaacs examines the standard approach to solving complex problems and to resolving communication issues aimed at reducing conflict in healthcare. This process involves bringing together a committee of highly qualified people who in turn assign *issues* to various sub-committees, which in turn report back to the whole committee. Following receipt of this collated information, these committees enter into a debate phase in an effort to reach a shared agreement followed by creation of an "action plan."[38] Dr. Isaacs refers to this approach as consensus building. As Dr. Isaacs concludes in his article, the purpose of a consensus approach (the root of the word means "to feel together") is to find a view that reflects what most people in a group can "live with for now."

Let us rejoin our fictional hospital meeting for a moment to examine how well the consensus approach will work to solve the conflict.

"Finally," fumes Dr. Steth, the chief hospital administrator, to himself. "We've been at this for four hours and all we have left to do is summarize our study-group findings, seek the recommendation that fits within the budget, and get out of here! I'm sick of the infighting and chronic complaints. I'm sick of taking all the blame for everyone's shortcomings," he muses.

"Look," Dr. Steth says to the group, "we've been discussing the patient wait-time issue for four hours, and it's been studied to death over the past few months by our sub-committees. I want a show of hands in favour of the primary recommendation to create a secondary waiting room for admitted emergency patients awaiting ward admission. Further, I want this committee to approve a protocol for a guaranteed three-hour wait time for these patients to any available bed in any of our wards."

Everyone inwardly sighs. Senior Nurse Jane Marrow speaks up expressing thoughts probably shared by all. "Look, we've been around and around the table with our input. This looks like the best option within the budget and staffing problems we have. Let's just go with it! Put in the sub-waiting room and start moving those patients into the wards! At least that will put an end to the ugly confrontations with patients in the main waiting room. It's so bad I can't bring myself to work out there any-more—televisions blaring, angry patients, distressed families—it's unbelievable how terrible things are. This solution isn't perfect, but at least it might work for now."

"All right, all right," responds Dr. Steth. "Let's get this done. It looks like we have a consensus, unless anyone else has anything to add."

"Just get me out of here," thinks Nurse Jane Marrow to herself. "I'm counting the days to early retirement. If this works for the next two years, I'm out of here, and it's somebody else's problem!"

So, we have a consensus, probably leading to a "solution" that will seem to work for a while. But, asks Dr. Isaacs, have the solutions, the consensus, altered the "fundamental patterns that led people to disagree at the outset?" Has the group actually addressed the underlying etiology of the conflicts and changed the actual dynamics of future interactions? Perhaps not, if, as Dr. Isaacs suggests, committee members have failed to "consciously participate in the creation of shared meaning" through the discovery of common interests and shared needs.

How can shared meaning be achieved in a complex scientific environment such as healthcare? Even if it can be achieved is it worth the effort? What long-term solution does the achievement of shared meaning have for the problems bedevilling conflict and communication issues in the hospital environment? Below, we address the critical importance of the group achieving shared understanding of issues in order to create options for resolving conflicts.

The creation of "shared meaning" is not an impossible, ephemeral goal nor does it require special gifts. As Dr. Isaacs suggests, almost any group seeking a solution to a conflict can uncover a shared meaning. The process involves a *skill-set* that leads to the development of options for mutual gain based on the uncovering of hidden, often subconscious interests or needs driving the conflict and the achievement of goals or solutions that address these interests. The process does not begin with the pre-existing assumption that parties in conflict have conflicting goals nor does it seek to achieve consensus through whittling away of the desires of each party until the lowest common denominator is found. Rather the goal of interest-based conflict resolution (achieving shared meaning) is to practise problem-solving strategies that focus on joint mutual gain—a third option, in essence, that actively addresses the underlying interests of each party in the conflict. The success of achieving shared meaning is the creation of solutions that fully respond to the *needs* and *interests* of the parties—not their *positions*.

What is the difference between a position and an interest? Why does it matter that the interest-based conflict resolution process seeks to uncover the latter rather than the former? To analyze this, let us examine a fictional meeting involving an attending staff physician, a senior resident, and the preceptor/program director for the senior resident.

Dr. Cortex, department head for internal medicine at Mercy West Faculty of Medicine, opens the door to his office waiting room on a dreary, drizzly Monday morning. "Surprise, surprise. Here sits Dr. Frontal Lobe and Dr. Humerous—back again with their ongoing, vitriolic, and never-ending conflict," he thinks to himself. "These two are like oil floating on water—unmixable. I should never agree to meet with them first thing on a Monday morning. It just ruins the whole week," he grumbles to himself.

"All right," he says with a forced smile to the two waiting physicians, "what can I do for you two today?"

Dr. Frontal Lobe, the junior staff physician in oncology, speaks first. "My position is final, Dr. Cortex. I demand an apology from Dr. Humerous and his promise that he will stop undermining my authority in front of junior residents who report to me."

Dr. Humerous, the division head and staff physician, snorts in reply. "You know I'm not apologizing. Dr. Frontal Lobe deserved what she got! A full review of her treatment protocol for that diabetic patient on rounds yesterday. The junior residents on rounds with us needed to hear my opinions, and I'm not in the least bit sorry for airing them—patient well-being comes first. My position is that I will never offer an apology for delivering excellence in healthcare. *My* position is final—no apology. And Dr. Frontal Lobe had better understand that I will correct her whenever necessary. Furthermore, I don't care who is listening when I tell her she is wrong. She needs to toughen up and improve her skills if she wants to work at this hospital!"

The foregoing fictional exchange reflects classic positional bargaining and positional conflict. Each party has a final position—their final solution to the conflict:

- Dr. Frontal Lobe demands an apology and a commitment from Dr. Humerous that he will stop undermining her authority in front of junior residents.

- Dr. Humerous refuses to provide an apology and wants Dr. Frontal Lobe to accept negative feedback and to learn from her mistakes.

These positions seemingly have no shared meaning and no underlying common interests. The conflict appears intractable: a clash of personalities. But is it? Should the department head probe deeper to determine the unstated interests of Dr. Frontal Lobe and

Dr. Humerous, as outlined in Maslow's Hierarchy of Needs? Proponents of the principled communication process would answer with a resounding "Yes! Dr. Frontal Lobe and Dr. Humerous must seek principled dialogue in which they uncover common interests." There is hope for a final resolution of the clash of these two personalities, utilizing an interest-based approach to conflict resolution. This approach is discussed further in the next chapter.

Talking Points

i) There may be no real dialogue, no addressing of underlying interests, and no principled communication in a collective sense occurring in many interactions between healthcare professionals.

ii) The application of rational, credible, widely practised cognitive processes utilized by physicians and nurses in the diagnosis and treatment of patients and the creation of protocols for resolution of conflict may simply add to and perpetuate problems of negative communication. Such failures occur because these seemingly rational processes do not identify and address the underlying interests and needs of the parties to the conflict. In failing to identify and address needs, the conflict continues.

iii) Parties to conflict must work to discover their needs and work in a principled manner to uncover common needs and interests. The process is a skill-set leading to a development of options for mutual gain based on uncovering of hidden, often subconscious interests or needs driving the conflict and the achievement of goals or solutions that address these interests—shared meaning. ∎

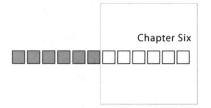

Chapter Six

Communication Tools
for Interest-based
Conflict Resolution

C onflict can be defined to include all words and actions involving an "expressed struggle between two or more interdependent parties arising from a real or *perceived* difference in needs or values."[39] Conflict is a natural product of the dynamics of intersecting needs whether in the workplace, in personal relationships, or between nations. Conflict or the potential for conflict lies in the shadows of every human interaction.

Given that healthcare professionals cannot entirely remove conflict from the workplace, and thereby avoid its potential effect on the work environment, it is incumbent upon physicians, nurses, and hospital administrators to become familiar with and utilize the tools of principled communication.

But what does it mean to become a principled communicator? And how can we remain principled when engaged in conflict with workplace bullies, passive-aggressive personalities, conflict avoiders, or those whose power clearly exceeds ours?

In the seminal work on principled communication, *Getting to Yes* by Roger Fisher, William Ury, and Bruce Patton,[40] the authors examine conflict from three perspectives:

- The people engaged in the conflict

- The problem driving the conflict

- The process of communication

Fisher, Ury, and Patton urge parties to examine conflict as a series of interactions arranged along the grid of a triangle consisting of the people, the problem, and the process. This approach allows parties in conflict to facilitate a clear, concise analysis of the origins of the conflict and come to a consensus regarding the action needed to move forward to resolve the conflict.

When a conflict is broken down in this manner, parties gain the immediate psychological advantage of breaking a "large" problem into smaller parts. Each part of the conflict can be addressed separately and different solutions can be addressed through the process of brainstorming options for solutions to each aspect of the conflict.

Diagrammatically illustrated, the *Conflict Triangle* can be depicted in the following manner:

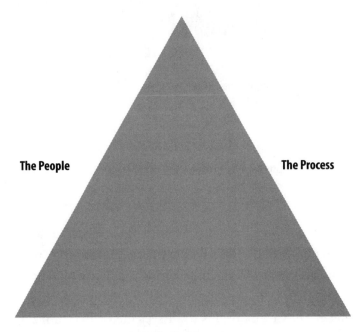

The People

The Process

The Problem

Aligned along each axis of the Conflict Triangle, Fisher, Ury, and Patton list the various sources of conflict as they relate to the *people* in the conflict, the *problem* to be resolved, and the *process* used by the people to resolve the problem.

When conflict is viewed in this manner, we can begin to analyze the causes as part of a system. We can step away from the linear cause and effect approach, e.g., "He unjustly criticized my work. I refuse to be on his team going forward!" to development of a more neutral frame—the triangle—within which to analyze the conflict.

Fully described schematically, the Conflict Triangle looks like this:

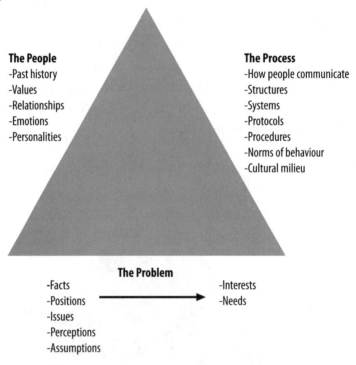

The People
-Past history
-Values
-Relationships
-Emotions
-Personalities

The Process
-How people communicate
-Structures
-Systems
-Protocols
-Procedures
-Norms of behaviour
-Cultural milieu

The Problem
-Facts
-Positions
-Issues
-Perceptions
-Assumptions

-Interests
-Needs

Utilizing the Conflict Triangle to sharpen our focus, let us return to the potentially unpleasant meeting between Dr. Humerous and Dr. Frontal Lobe in Dr. Cortex's office. At first glance it would appear that there is no easy solution to this clash of personalities. But what if Dr. Cortex begins to dissect the conflict utilizing the Conflict Triangle with a series of questions designed to separate the people from the problem? Let us return to the dialogue that *might* now occur:

Dr. Cortex: "Dr. Humerous, from what you have said so far, I understand that you are concerned with the *process* by which Dr. Frontal Lobe communicates with you when there is a question or concern on her part with patient care. Am I correct?"

Dr. Humerous: "Yes, that's it, exactly. I feel exceptionally stressed and unfairly singled out when Dr. Frontal Lobe challenges my orders in front of others, especially junior residents and nursing staff."

Dr. Cortex: "But am I correct in concluding that you and Dr. Frontal Lobe are equally committed to providing a high quality of patient care?"

Dr. Frontal Lobe: "Yes, of course!"

Dr. Humerous: "That goes without saying! Actually the main reason I outlined my concern about insulin protocol for that patient last week in front of other residents was because of my ongoing frustration in communication with Dr. Frontal Lobe. I am never sure where she is when she is on call."

Dr. Frontal Lobe: "But that's because Dr. Humerous doesn't respond to text messages."

Dr. Cortex: "So Dr. Frontal Lobe and Dr. Humerous, am I stating the problem correctly: part of the problem is the *mode* of communication about patient care? Do we need to devise a protocol for communication that you are *both* comfortable with?"

Dr. Frontal Lobe: "Yes, in fact I would be more than happy to show Dr. Humerous how I text-message and the fastest way to get in touch with me."

Dr. Humerous: "I guess it is time for me to enter the twenty-first century. I agree that I need to learn how to text when necessary."

In this portion of the meeting, Dr. Cortex has begun to separate the people from the problem to allow the parties to identify the etiology of the conflict. Here, the conflict is about the *system* of communication between Dr. Humerous and Dr. Frontal Lobe. Dr. Frontal Lobe is comfortable with text-messaging. Dr. Humerous prefers personal contact. This conflict is less about inherent dislike between these physicians than it is about focusing on their mode of communication with each other. Much of their conflict may arise from the process of communication.

What techniques of communication can we utilize to understand and resolve conflict from the perspective of the Conflict Triangle? How do we separate the people from the problem? How do we get at underlying, often unstated interests and needs? How do we get people to focus on their common interests? How do we assist parties in conflict to move away from emotional disagreement toward a process of generating options for *mutual* gain? All of these questions can be addressed through the process of learning to "actively listen," to ask "open questions," to reframe a negative statement into a positive, to probe for underlying needs, and to brainstorm options for mutual gain.

Active Listening

The key to effective utilization of the Conflict Triangle is the ability to employ appropriate communication skills of assertive speaking, listening, questioning, reflecting, and reframing. This process is referred to as active listening. Active listening is not only the art of *hearing* but also *understanding* what is being said.[41]

Active listening requires the listener to confirm to the speaker two crucial things:

- That the speaker has been heard.

- That the speaker has been understood.

Let us examine each of the skills in turn.

Assertive Speaking

Effective communication requires the ability to convey verbal and non-verbal message(s) in a way that the other party can hear and understand. It means each party communicates in a clear manner their own interests and feelings. When involved in conflict it is important that the parties are able to disclose their own interests in a non-threatening way and that they are able to let others express their interests.

The language chosen to convey information/messages will impact how the information/message is heard. This is especially so in a conflict situation where it is important to speak in a positive and assertive manner. The speaker should convey clearly how they feel and what they think in an objective, non-confrontational manner. The speaker should speak only for themselves and should avoid speaking for the other or attributing feelings or thoughts to the other. The communication should be focused in the present and should avoid recycling the past.

Assertive communication involves the use of "I" language. The use of "I" statements helps the listener understand what feelings and reactions the speaker is experiencing. They also help the parties take ownership of their feelings and their part in the conflict. For example: "I cannot participate in this discussion when voices are being raised. If we could address issues in a calmer fashion I will be able to participate in this discussion," as opposed to: "You are causing these discussions to break down. I will not negotiate with you!"

Listening

Good listening involves paying attention to what is being said and to the non-verbal communication accompanying what is being said. The majority of what is being conveyed during communication is non-verbal and is done through body language, gestures, eye movements, facial expressions, and posture. In order to listen carefully we must also suspend judgment of what the person is saying and not think about what our response may be. Interruptions should also be avoided. Good listening requires undivided attention and listening not just with your ears but your whole body, exemplified by the use of non-verbal signals that indicate attention and interest and avoid those that mark disinterest.

Not only should the listener pay attention in order to actively listen, the listener should check the accuracy of the message with the speaker through the use of questioning, probing, and clarifying skills. Questioning, probing, and clarifying are used to ensure understanding and to let the speaker know that she has been heard and understood. By using these skills, the listener provides an opportunity for the speaker to clarify her meaning if there is misunderstanding.

Questioning

Questions generally fall into one of the following categories.

1. Open-ended questions

Open-ended questions allow for the broadest possible answer. They cannot be answered by a simple yes or no response. Open-ended questions are typically used to gather as much information about the conflict as possible, to identify parties' perceptions about the issues to be addressed, and to identify shared or common interests. Open-ended questions usually begin with one of the following:

- What ...

- Why ... (be careful how you use "why questions")

- How ...

- Where ...

- Who ...

- Explain ...

- Describe ...

- Help me understand ...

- Help me out here ...

Open questions can be further divided into:

Probing questions are used to dig beneath the statement. They seek information at a deeper level and generally encourage the speaker to elaborate. Their purpose is to learn about motivating objectives.

- Please tell me more about how you came to this conclusion?

- What is it about this that concerns you the most?

Clarifying questions seek to sharpen the listener's understanding. They involve thinking about what the person has said. If a comment is vague or inexact then it is necessary to clarify what the speaker has said. This can be done through the use of probing questions.

- What are the facts?

- Can you tell me more about that?

Justifying questions ask the speaker to give more evidence of the view expressed. They are used to point out inconsistencies to the speaker. Justifying questions must be used carefully to avoid putting the parties on the defensive as there is a risk that the speaker will feel challenged. They are best asked in a manner that seeks clarification or asks for help in understanding the different points of view expressed by the speaker as illustrated below.

- Last time we met you indicated that your staff was over-worked and needed more help and resources. Now you say that your department is running just fine and you would not like Dr. Scalpel to help out. I'm confused. What has changed?

- When we last spoke you did not wish to have the department head involved in this conversation. Now you are suggesting a formal meeting with the department head. How has your view on this changed?

Consequential questions seek to make a "reality test" and are used to explore future implications, test hypotheses, and determine the practicality of options and proposals. These questions tend to facilitate forward thinking and infuse creativity into the discussion.

- How do you see the future of this situation if this problem is not resolved now?

- How do you think your staff will respond to the proposed changes in their salary and their hours of work and how might that impact your department?

- How will this proposal address the joint concerns raised by the doctors and nurses in the ER?

If we examine an exchange between Dr. Venous and Dr. Artery we can observe the use of open questioning through probing and clarifying.

Dr. Venous, senior surgery resident, and Dr. Artery, junior resident, are involved in an intense discussion over central line protocol and technique.

Dr. Venous: "You just don't seem to be developing the necessary surgical skills, Dr. Artery. You don't seem to be confident enough to proceed with the insertion of the central line by yourself. I always have to come help you.

What's going on?"

Dr. Artery: "Can I just clarify what your particular concerns are with my technique? There was a problem last week with patient John Brown, and I acknowledge that I had to call you. But you advised at the time that the morbid obesity of the patient made it extraordinarily difficult to get the central line in. I've inserted at least five other central lines without calling you at all."

Dr. Venous: "Well, I was unaware that you have inserted five other central lines. My specific concern with the morbidly obese patient was your demeanour. You seemed uncertain to me. You frightened the patient on that day. He thought you didn't know what you were doing. Later he complained to the charge nurse!"

Dr. Artery: "Okay, I acknowledge that the patient might have been ill at ease. Are there any other patients of mine that you are concerned about?"

Dr. Venous: "No, I was unaware that five other procedures had gone ahead without difficulty. I have heard your explanation and accept it."

So what has transpired here? Dr. Venous has made some very general accusatory statements. Dr. Artery has clarified, narrowed, and focused Dr. Venous's concerns. He has asked probing questions in a neutral manner and has successfully pared down the general accusation to a specific patient on a specific day. Dr. Artery has separated people from the problem (central line protocol and procedure). What could have been an unresolved argument and an emotion-laden exchange with bad feelings on both sides has been resolved through clarification by Dr. Artery.

2. Closed questions

Closed questions are utilized to narrow the scope of inquiry, to assist the parties to focus, or to obtain concrete information. They should be avoided early in the conflict-resolution process because closed questions select the subject matter of the response and limit the scope of the reply. They generally seek a specific statement of fact.

Closed questions usually call for a succinct affirmation that the listener has correctly assimilated the information given by the speaker. Closed questions usually contain a summary of the information being imparted. They usually begin with phrases such as:

"Am I correct when I say that you have now told me about all of the concerns you have about your difficulties with ..."

"How fast was the car travelling when it entered the intersection ..."

"When did Dr. Doe ask you to see that patient ..."

Yes/no questions are utilized to ask the opposing party to confirm or deny the information contained within the question. Yes/no questions are a form of closed question.

3. Leading questions

Leading questions are a special category of closed question, typically used by lawyers in the trial process known as cross examination. The leading question contains within it the desired answer. Examples of leading questions include the following:

"Sir, would you agree with me that on the night of June 14, 2008, you were indeed at the pub?"

"Ma'am, may I suggest to you that all along you knew that Dick Doe was planning to hit John Doe on the head with the hammer?"

Leading questions are generally to be avoided outside of the trial scenario.

In summary, in the course of dialogue, open-ended questions should be utilized in the beginning in order to elicit underlying interests and to gather as much information as possible. As the parties work to frame the issues for their agenda and begin to probe one another for common interests, closed questions can be used to focus the discussion. The yes/no question should be limited, used only when specific information is required. Leading questions should be avoided in an interest-based dialogue.

Diagrammatically represented:[42]

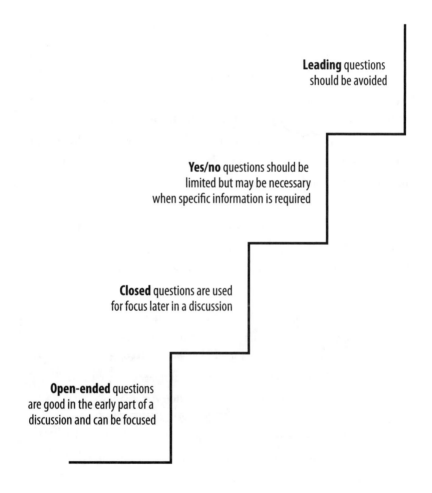

Leading questions
should be avoided

Yes/no questions should be
limited but may be necessary
when specific information is required

Closed questions are used
for focus later in a discussion

Open-ended questions
are good in the early part of a
discussion and can be focused

Reflecting

Not only is it important for effective communication to ask open-ended questions, it is also important to check the accuracy of the parties' understanding of the message being conveyed through a series of speaking techniques that are often referred to as **reflective** skills. These skills are used to ensure understanding and let the parties know they have been heard and understood. Reflecting skills include paraphrasing and reframing.

Paraphrasing is an equally effective tool for communication in the Conflict Triangle and is utilized to cool down emotional content while conveying understanding of the speaker's content or feelings or both. It involves distilling the information and emotion from the speaker's statement and then conveying back that the speaker has been heard and understood. Effective paraphrasing reflects *empathy*: a significant catalyst in the process of conflict resolution. It also reduces negativity in the speaker's statements.

Let us look at a fictitious exchange that demonstrates the process of the paraphrase. The exchange involves two junior residents, Dr. Cardio and Dr. Lumbar, arguing over a call schedule. They are meeting with their senior resident, who is skilled in the art of paraphrase.

> Dr. Cardio, junior resident, addressing the senior resident: "Dr. Graft, I'm so incredibly tired I can barely keep my eyes open! This is my eighteenth hour on duty, and I have to finish the charting! The rotation schedule you've set for next month is unfair. I have two kids and I've missed birthdays, hockey games, and holidays. I know I have to do the rotations as you set them, but you just have to understand that I need to spend *some* weekends with my kids. I want at least a couple of weekends in the next thirty days."

> Dr. Lumbar: "Look, I object to favouritism in setting the call schedules. I don't have kids. I like and respect Dr. Cardio, but I am just as overworked as he is and I would like a weekend off too. I have a fiancé who never sees me!"
>
> Dr. Graft, senior resident: "So Dr. Cardio and Dr. Lumbar, I can see that you are both fatigued and frustrated with the on-call schedule that I have set for the next thirty days. Both of you want some weekend time off, albeit for different reasons. Am I correct?"
>
> Dr. Cardio and Dr. Lumbar simultaneously: "Yes!"
>
> Dr. Graft: "So, would you agree that perhaps if the two of you sit down together you can arrive at a solution to the problem? We have only a limited number of residents to meet the call schedule. If you both need some time off perhaps you can work out a solution that will accommodate your mutual interests? Why don't the two of you have a short discussion over coffee and come back to see me this afternoon with your proposal?"

In this fictitious exchange, Dr. Graft has utilized a paraphrase to reflect empathy and understanding, which neutralized some of the negative expressions of emotion. In addition, he has catalyzed the parties to begin to work together to create a solution to the conflict.

Reframing is one of the most effective tools of communicating. Once perfected, the reframe can be used to solve many seemingly intractable conflicts.

People who find themselves in conflict often use language that is judgmental, positional, and biased toward a subjective view. Through reframing, the language of the parties can be translated into neutral terms. An effective reframe can help identify the underlying need or concern of the speaker while changing a positional negative statement into a positive problem-solving statement.

In essence, the reframe is a paraphrased statement about a problem or issue that allows the parties to view the problem in a different light. It is a response that limits and reshapes the message to make it more constructive. The effective reframe reshapes the parties' perception of one another in a manner that moves the dialogue forward toward understanding and resolution. Reframe removes blame, judgment, bias, and position. It identifies underlying needs and common interests.

We reframe to:

1. Allow the participants to hear and understand one another.

2. Permit the parties to work on an agenda that is reflective of their interests.

3. Allow the parties to begin the process of generating options for mutual gain.

A reframe can be utilized to:

A. Change a position to an interest:

Position: "I am not working these hours for so little pay!"

Reframe: "So fair compensation is very important to you?"

B. Change a judgment to a question:

Judgment: "I don't trust him. He never does what he is supposed to do."

Reframe: "So you would like some reassurance that Joe will follow through?"

C. Change a blame to a need:

Blame: "He is completely unreliable."

Reframe: "You need reassurance of reliability."

D. Change a past concern to a future resolution:

Statement: "I have had it with the last-minute changes to the schedule! I am sick of changing plans for my weekends at the last minute."

Reframe: "So you would like to create a schedule that you can rely on?"

E. Change an individual problem to a shared concern:

Statement: "Everyone at this meeting thinks I enjoy being in charge of endeavouring to resolve all the staff administration issues! In fact, the extra money I receive just isn't worth it anymore. I am sick of all the complaining!"

Reframe: "So you would like to see a more collaborative approach to resolving these human resource issues?"

An effective reframe:

- Identifies the interests expressed by the parties in a negative statement.

- Flips the negative aspect of the statement to make a positive statement.

Statement: We talk and talk and go nowhere.

Interests: Finality, efficiency, and productivity

Reframe: I understand that you are frustrated with this process and that you would like to have more structure to our discussions so that they may be more productive. What would make this process more productive for you?

The reframe is perhaps the most difficult communication tool to master. It requires practice, practice, practice! However, once the skill is acquired, the results can be amazing in overcoming barriers to resolution of conflict. Let us return to the emergency department of ABC Hospital to observe the reframe in use during the course of a meeting of hospital administrators, nurses, and a "difficult" physician, Dr. Femur. The meeting concerns numerous complaints to administration about Dr. Femur's "bedside" manner and her clinical interaction with nursing staff and residents. Dr. Femur has raised issues of her own including inefficiency, department overcrowding, lack of proper clinical training for nursing staff, and disrespectful conduct of residents.

The meeting is being facilitated by an independent faciliator, Mr. Barbeau, who is skilled in the art of the "reframe." Our meeting has just convened and the parties are outlining their positions. Mr. Barbeau is endeavouring to uncover underlying needs and interests in order to create an agenda. The meeting is taking place in a bright, sunny room with a view of the mountains. Fortunately, the table at which the parties are seated is round!

Mr. Barbeau, the facilitator: "I would like to hear from each party in a brief opening statement. Please feel free to speak frankly. I would ask each party to allow others to speak without interruption. Everyone will have an equal opportunity to be heard. Nurse I.V., as head nurse, would you like to go first?"

Nurse I.V.: "I have been nursing for twenty years. I thought I had encountered every kind of difficult personality *until* I encountered Dr. Femur! My mandate to lead the nursing staff in a professional working environment has been completely undermined by Dr. Femur. I hate pointing fingers, but in my view her personality is a negative force affecting the morale of the entire nursing staff. Dr. Femur takes everything to a personal level."

Mr. Barbeau: [changing blame to need] "So, Nurse I.V., am I correct when I hear you that professional communication and interaction between nursing staff and physicians in

---

emergency is of primary importance for you as head nurse?"

Nurse I.V.: "Yes!"

Dr. Femur: "Well, I am amazed to hear that Nurse I.V. values professional interaction. I do too and, in my view, nursing staff—particularly junior staff—don't know the meaning of the word! I've had it with their petty grievances, their constant coffee breaks, and their poor attitude. Of course I've lost my temper with these people. My goodness, some of them don't even look like nurses—at least not the way they looked when I graduated from medicine in 1978!"

Mr. Barbeau: [changing a past concern to a future resolution] So, Dr. Femur, you too value a professional appearance and demeanour of staff in the emergency department. Do I understand you to say that you would be happy working in an emergency department that reflects those qualities?"

Dr. Femur: "Absolutely!"

In this initial exchange, we see the reframe being utilized to put a different focus on the conflict. The facilitator has identified common needs (professional demeanour, professional interaction) and has separated blame and criticism from the problem. We can expect the dialogue to move forward to allow the parties to identify ways and means of defining professional conduct for their future interaction.

Talking Points

i) Conflict is best viewed as a series of interactions arranged along the grid of a triangle consisting of the people, the problem, and the process. This perspective allows parties in conflict to facilitate a clear, concise analysis of the origins of the conflict and pinpoint with accuracy the action necessary to move forward to resolve the conflict.

ii) Parties to conflict must learn the art of assertive speaking, active listening, questioning, reflecting, and reframing in order to determine and understand the causes of conflict.

iii) The skill of reframing a negative statement into a positive is essential to the process of conflict resolution. The effective reframe:

- Identifies the interests underlying the speaker's statement.

- Flips the negative into a positive, focusing on future potential for resolution. ■

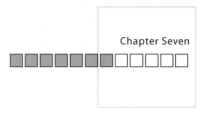

Chapter Seven

Barriers to Communication

Although most healthcare professionals are fairly accomplished communicators, many of them have incorporated destructive modes of communication[43] into everyday patterns of communication. Destructive modes of communication include criticizing, commanding, moralizing, telling others what to do, arguing, and interrupting. They may also include more complex patterns such as deception, manipulation, and strategic dialogue. These destructive patterns of communication may be amplified when we find ourselves in conflict situations.

To the extent communication in healthcare is destructive or deceptive, manipulative or even strategic, the quality of healthcare provided to patients may be adversely affected. By *deceptive* and *manipulative* we do not mean to imply *mal fides* (bad faith) on the part of the speaker—rather we mean that there is:

- an absence of principled, open, and honest interaction between parties to a communication

- a lack of awareness of the interests of others

- a lack of authenticity of engagement in the encounter

Barriers to meaningful dialogue of understanding may occur despite the best intentions of the parties to the communication. In communication we can divide these barriers into the following three categories:

1. Barriers of ego/identity or "face"

2. Barriers of emotion

3. Barriers of cognition

We shall examine each in turn.

Barriers of Ego/Identity

In the book *Difficult Conversations,* by Harvard Professors Doug Stone, Bruce Patton, and Sheila Heen, the authors identify matters of ego (in the Freudian[44] sense of the word) as a critically important barrier to dialogue. The reason, according to Stone et al, is that parties to conflict first examine conflict or an issue in communication from the perspective of the following question: What does the conflict, the issue, the problem *say about me?*

In order to examine this barrier, let us listen in on the following fictitious exchange between two nurses at the Emergency Department of ABC Hospital.

> Nurse A, a senior RN head nurse with twenty years experience has been confronted by Nurse B, who has recently graduated with a B.Sc. in nursing. The problem centres on a patient, Mr. Abcess, who is writhing in pain at triage. Mr. Abcess is clutching the lower right quadrant of his abdomen, sweating profusely, and yelling at anyone who endeavours to examine him.
>
> Nurse B: "I am really concerned about this patient. I think he might have retro-cecal appendicitis. If the appendix

> ruptures, he could die before we get him into surgery!"
>
> Nurse A (thinking to himself): "What an egotistical nurse! B.Sc., B.Sc. Big deal. So she had four years of university. She doesn't have the *authority* to make any diagnosis—that is the job of our attending physician. I don't care what she thinks. Furthermore, I don't like her tone of voice—disrespectful to me and to my twenty years of practical experience in the emergency department."
>
> Nurse B: Droning on and on … interrupting the thoughts of Nurse A.
>
> Nurse A: "Look Nurse B, we are just nurses, we do not make diagnoses. We will just have to wait until the doctor is able to see him. We are backed up. As usual!"

So, what is happening here? Is Nurse B truly communicating with Nurse A? Is any dialogue occurring? Is any attempt being made by Nurse B to alert the attending emergency physician or the senior resident to a potentially serious medical emergency? Has the level of triage changed? Probably not, as Nurse A is conducting an internal conversation with his ego! He is defending his own experience, is offended by the direct approach of a junior nurse, and although he will not admit it—even to himself—Nurse A is feeling insecure and perhaps a little jealous of the education and youth of Nurse B. For all of those reasons, the ego or "face needs" of Nurse A are acting as a *barrier* to communication between the two nurses and to the detriment of the patient.

Whether we are employees, employers, independent contractors, or professionals, we all hold ourselves to certain internal standards of behaviour and belief. These unstated internal codes often create multiple barriers to communication with others *and* to resolution of conflict as we perceive conflict from the following perspective: "What does the problem say about me?"

Ego or "face saving" is a major concern for people at times

but even more so when in conflict or when they are negotiating a resolution to a conflict. The concept of "face" refers to how we perceive ourselves and how we want others to see us. These concepts relate back to the interests discussed in Chapter Three. Having one's "face needs" met may be an interest underlying a position or may be what is driving the conflict.

There are two kinds of face needs: positive and negative. Positive face is the desire to belong, to have the approval of others, and to be seen as a particular type of person. Negative face is the desire for autonomy, not to be coerced or imposed upon by others. Threats to identity or loss of face occur when a person's self-image is challenged or ignored. This in turn produces behaviour designed to save or restore face. The communication then moves away from resolving the substance of the conflict and toward saving face. This may manifest itself in a refusal to step back from a position or create a need to avoid unjust intimidation. People's behaviour in this situation may be familiar strategies to save face, such as focusing blame on others, justifying their own behaviour, or making excuses. Or it may be less obvious, such as refusing to back off a position for fear of being perceived as weak or foolish. In any event, these behaviours may have serious implications for resolving a conflict situation as they will create a distraction from focusing on the substantive issues. The possible impacts include increased issues, decreased flexibility, or inclusion of others outside of the conflict to address the face concerns.

The ego or identity barrier is the most difficult to transcend as it leads to the following conundrum in conflict, according to Stone et al:

> If you, the other party in a conflict, want to change my mind, you must first seek to understand my inner voice, you must seek to engage me in a conversation with myself, you must demonstrate an understanding of my inner interests and needs.

Because of our deeply held beliefs, our assumptions determine how we make sense of conflict and how we decide to engage in or attempt to resolve conflict. Our ego or face often limits our perspective and our capacity to seek solutions to conflict. In *Difficult Conversations*, Stone et al identify the barrier of ego or face that may lead to five unproductive thinking habits:

1. We assume we are right.

2. We see ourselves as more reasonable than others.

3. We assign negative attributes and motives to others.

4. We hold others accountable for problems.

5. We avoid upsetting situations.

So how do we cross the barrier of ego in order to engage in dialogue with others? Stone et al advise that before we can negotiate with others to resolve conflict, we must negotiate first with our own internal voice (the ego).

How do we negotiate with ourselves? The first step is to be aware that we engage in these cognitive biases or unproductive thinking patterns. Parties to communication must recognize that judging, defending, daydreaming, and justifying all act as barriers. It requires recognition that we do not necessarily know *all* of the facts, and that we do not necessarily know the *correct* solution to the problem.

In summary, we begin to listen:

- When we realign our internal voice toward curiosity.

- When we recognize our internal bias and move beyond it.

In order to cross the ego barrier, the following may be helpful:

- Set up an exchange of information based on objective data.

- Ask the party who is limited by the ego barrier to "future gaze." E.g., "Where do you see our conflict going in the future? How do you envision the future in the event we continue in this manner?"

- Role Play. Have the parties or the other party change sides. Each party to the conflict assumes the role of a different party to the conflict and tries to view the situation from that party's perception.

Barriers of Emotion

Conflicts, whether chronic and ongoing, or acute and sudden, contain within them emotional elements—anger, fear, frustration, and impatience—to name a few. Emotion in conflict is experienced in our bodies as well as our minds.[45] The Anger Arousal Cycle, described below, depicts the progress of anger and its negative effect on the quality of our judgment.[46]

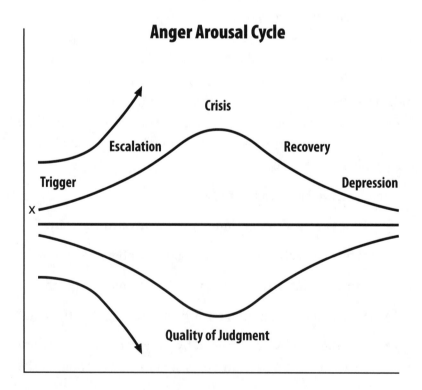

Anger Arousal Cycle

Crisis

Escalation   Recovery

Trigger   Depression

X

Quality of Judgment

During the escalation phase, adrenaline is released into the bloodstream. Respiration, heart rate, and blood pressure may increase. Muscles tense and pupils enlarge. As anger escalates to crisis, cognitive skills are adversely affected. The capacity to reason, to focus on issues, and to brainstorm for collaborative solutions is significantly reduced. "Chemicals like adrenaline, cortisol, dopamine, serotonin and oxytocin create and accompany emotions and profoundly affect our ability to perceive and recall what happens when we are in dispute."[47]

While we are in a state of anger, the rational mind—located in the neocortex of the brain—does not prevail over the secretion of adrenaline from the amygdala. This physiological phenomenon influences our perception, memory, and ability to engage in dialogue.

Barriers of Cognition/Attribution Theory

In conflict, not only do we experience negative emotion ourselves but we also assume that others with whom we are in conflict are acting out of negative emotion or intent in their actions toward us. In an article written for the Harvard Business School Publishing Corporation, Bill Noonan examines how attribution theory—our assumptions of negative intent and ill-will in others—often lead to our incorrect assignment of negative motives, negative emotions, or even serious character flaws in others.[48]

Attributions are the beliefs or hypotheses we all form about the underlying motivation for our own behaviour and other's behaviour. Attributions play a large role in the escalation of conflict in the workplace and thus have the potential to undermine effective communication and conflict resolution.

Attribution theory[49] is based on two premises:

1. We interpret behaviour according to its causes (why did they do that?). These causes are either:

    -   internal (disposition/character-related)

    -   or external (situational)

2. Our causal explanations, as explained in premise 1 above, affect our reactions to the behaviour.

Our interpretation of the cause of a particular behaviour is influenced by two biases:

1. We commonly attribute the behaviour of others to internal factors (character related), and we commonly attribute our own behaviour to situational factors. This is especially the case for behaviour we believe to be intentional and goal driven. In conflict situations attributions about the motives of the other party are likely to be negative.

2. We defensively attribute the negative consequences of our own actions to situational factors and the positive consequences to ourselves. This is especially likely to occur in situations involving success or failure.

Once made, attributions are very difficult to change. In part this is because we are unaware that it has even occurred. Even as we start to become aware of others' attributions, it is very difficult to see our own. They seem correct, and they are self-reinforcing.

Attributions affect conflict in several ways. Negative attribution can become a serious barrier to dialogue, to collaborative action, and to resolution of conflict as parties in conflict often do not test the reality of their assumptions and perceptions. Negative attribution in the healthcare context can have a serious impact on the quality of care provided to patients. Decisions may be made and courses of action undertaken based on perceptions and assumptions as to the intent of co-workers and superiors, often with no attempt made to test their accuracy.

To illustrate the foregoing, let us examine the inner thoughts of two senior attending orthopaedic specialists, Dr. Yes and Dr. No, attending a meeting to redesign the protocol for delivery of medical service in the Department of Orthopaedics at ENG Hospital. The meeting has been called by the department head on an urgent basis as a result of complaints by both senior and junior residents over conflicting orders given by the two specialists.

Dr. Yes is thirty-five years old. She is viewed by most residents as brilliant and innovative. She spearheaded the recent changes to patient protocol. She is technologically savvy: completely at ease with internet applications, mobile handsets, and electronic medical record protocols.

The meeting begins. Let us examine Dr. No's inner thoughts:

"I know Dr. Yes thinks that I am an old curmudgeon! She has probably introduced these new patient-care initiatives just to force me into early retirement. I just know Dr. Yes has no respect for my thirty years of clinical experience. I believe she is laughing at me behind my back because I can't use email and other fancy technologies. Of course I am losing my temper! It is because it is the only way that I can be heard anymore. Admitting that I don't know all this internet 'lingo' is a sure sign of weakness."

Meanwhile, let us "listen in" on Dr. Yes's inner thoughts:

"Dr. No is impossible! He never takes time for any social interaction. I think he fails to respect the female orthopaedic residents—after all, he is a product of the 1970s medical school culture. I just know he doesn't like me even though I have tried to include him in our protocols. He will never come onside. He is biased! My only recourse is to force him out of the decision-making loop."

Given the negative attribution, how productive is the meeting with the department head going to be? Will there be any true collaboration between Dr. No and Dr. Yes? Not unless the department head is able to provide an opportunity for Dr. No and Dr. Yes to voice, test, and determine the accuracy of the other side's perceptions.

Dr. Able, the department head, can make Dr. No and Dr. Yes aware that we all have the tendency to make negative attributions, especially in conflict situations. He can then encourage the doctors as suggested by Stone et al in their book *Difficult Conversations* [50] to disentangle "intention" from "impact" of the behaviour or statement. They remind us that although we can know the impact of others' actions, we cannot know their intention.

Roger Fisher, William Ury, and Bruce Patton, Harvard law professors and authors of the seminal text on conflict resolution *Getting to Yes*, examine a number of very effective solutions when people (or rather their negative attributions toward one another) are the problem in conflict.[51]

1. The parties in conflict must consciously and jointly create a process for sharing their views about the conflict. Facilitators and mediators define this process as the creation of "ground rules." Ground rules must be created jointly by the parties to conflict, never imposed by any one party upon the other. Ground rules provide the skeletal structure for collaborative decision making. They include giving equal opportunities for each party to speak uninterrupted with respect to their view of the issues, the setting of time limits for the process, the creation and prioritizing of items on the agenda, ensuring each party's equal access to facts and collateral information, and the creation of equal opportunities for deciding the timing of and location of the meetings.

2. The emotion of each party should be uncovered and expressed. Resentment, frustration, and anger often dwell within the inner thoughts of individuals in conflict, acting as

catalysts to its resolution. Facilitators and/or mediators who are brought in to help the parties resolve conflict can provide a safe and secure opportunity for parties in conflict to engage in venting of emotion. The revelation of emotion underpinning the conflict is the first step toward its deconstruction and resolution.

3. The parties must be given an opportunity to uncover their own needs and interests and test the accuracy of their own perceptions about the interests and needs of the other parties to the conflict.

4. The parties to conflict must, in joint session, identify the source of mistrust and must jointly discuss specific actions to be taken to overcome these sources. Mistrust can never be the unidentified "elephant in the room," impeding resolution of the conflict. No matter how difficult it is to talk about, the reason behind mistrust must be disclosed and discussed before long-lasting collaborative solutions to the conflict can be achieved.[52]

Talking Points

i) Emotions, attribution of negative intent, and ego act as barriers to resolution of conflict.

ii) The parties to conflict can overcome these barriers with the help of a mediator or facilitator who will assist the parties to create a safe environment for venting emotion, exploring causes of mistrust, and revealing interests underlying the positions of the parties in conflict.

iii) The parties to conflict can overcome cognitive barriers such as attributions and ego/face issues by being aware that they exist and that these biases are predictable and can generally occur with all parties to negotiation.

iv) The most important technique to manage attributions is to be aware that we all have the tendency to make them. In the book *Difficult Conversations* the authors suggest that it is important to disentangle intention from impact.[53] They remind us that although we can know the impact of others' actions, we cannot know their intention. This is another area where effective communication is vital.

The most effective way to deal with face loss or ego issues is to be mindful of these issues and prevent them from occurring in the first place. Avoid taking rigid positions in negotiations and when engaging in discussions or negotiations:

- Be civil.

- Be respectful.

- Be thoughtful and pro-active rather than reactive.

- Use person-centred speech rather than position-centred speech. Avoid blaming, judgmental, or evaluative language.

- Speak for yourself and not the other person.

- Utilize questions to seek information and clarify assumptions.

- Make requests rather than demands. ■

Chapter Eight

Overcoming Barriers to Principled Communication

Dr. B., the outside expert in healthcare communication, strides into the convened meeting of physicians and administrators with a renewed sense of purpose. He clutches his PowerPoint presentation to his chest. He is so pleased with it! He just knows that all of the personnel problems within the unit will be resolved once everyone sees the presentation he has prepared. It identifies the various sources of the conflict, the cause of the conflict, the cause of the inefficiencies, and the plan for solving declining staff morale. The pre-printed agenda prepared by Dr. B. matches the PowerPoint outline. It is brilliant!

If people just look at the agenda and watch the presentation, Dr. B. knows that everyone will come to the realization that he is right about everything that is plaguing the unit.

Mandated changes to organizations implemented through "top-down" memorandum, PowerPoint presentations, mass email, or as the aftermath of team leader retreats often fail to achieve their intended effect in restoring harmony or maintaining long-lasting change in the workplace.

Often workers return to the old way of doing things and conflict continues unresolved. Chronic communication breakdown festers beneath the surface of workplace relationships. Why is this?

Recent research into the dynamics of workplace conflict indicate that permanent positive change in the channels of communication leading to conflict resolution can only be achieved if the "core group" desires solutions to the conflict and *creates* the process for implementation of those solutions.

In his book *Who Really Matters: The Core Group Theory of Power, Privilege and Success,* Art Kleiner defines the core group in any organization as a group of individuals who have the power, influence, and knowledge to become catalysts for change.[54]

In order to implement long-lasting solutions to chronic conflict and communication breakdown in a large complex environment, such as healthcare, it is essential to identify who the core group is *and* to ensure that they become the driving force for change.

But how do we identify who the core group really is? Where does the real power to effect change exist in day-to-day communication? In an individual? Within a team? At the top of hierarchy or at its base? How do we engender the support of its members? How do we determine who has the real power to create change in the day-to-day communication within the workplace and to finally resolve chronic conflict?

In order to illustrate the importance of asking those questions, let us return to our fictitious scenario.

Dr. Patella, senior resident, watches with dismay as another outside "expert" speaker enters the room. "Oh great!" she thinks. "Another PowerPoint presentation. Did I drink enough coffee this morning in order to stay awake through this interminable meeting? Another expert from administration who is going to give us all the benefit of his wisdom! He knows nothing about what is really wrong with our department and of course he isn't aware of Dr. Blood's arrogance and the games he plays with residents and nursing staff. They can do an infinite number of flow charts and PowerPoints, but until things change significantly with Dr. Blood nothing will change for the better in our department. We'll all just continue our daily dance around Dr. Blood. Whatever is decided here won't matter. Dr. Blood's conduct in our unit is the real problem!"

If we examine the foregoing meeting, the following questions should arise: Who possesses the real power to effect change in day-to-day communication? Is it Dr. Blood? Is it Dr. Patella and her peer group? Is it hospital administration? Is it our PowerPoint expert speaker? In other words, who is the core group?

Identification of the core group and, more significantly, catalyzing the core group to incorporate principled dialogue into the dynamic and network of communication requires more than team leader retreats, hiring outside experts, and generating memoranda for change.

1. "There are two criteria underlying an individual's decision to cooperate [in communication]: the degree of responsibility and the efficacy of contribution" within the communication network.[55]

In other words, individual workers will decide to cooperate if they feel that their process of communication matters and that they have true responsibility for how the workplace functions day-to-day.

2. The actual structure of the communication network will profoundly impact the degree of cooperation amongst the core group as a whole in maintaining the communication network and resolving conflict.

If a large complex community such as healthcare desires to implement long-lasting change to the manner in which it communicates within itself and to introduce principled dialogue, the core group must be identified and catalyzed to create solutions to conflict. If not, the core group itself will become an internal structural barrier to the introduction of principled communication.

To successfully introduce to the core group a change in the dynamic of communication, with the goal of reducing conflict, a model of communication must be introduced that motivates the core group to work collectively, not only within itself but with others outside the group.

Creating a desire for solving conflict within the core group may initially require counterintuitive action within the hierarchy. By this we mean that the normal protocols for implementation of change in the workplace may have to be abandoned. The organization must become open to allowing the core group to decide what it needs to do to improve workplace interaction, to take responsibility for creating a process of resolving conflict and implementing its own *long-lasting* solutions.

It is important to recognize that counterintuitive moves are often initially uncomfortable and stressful. However, participants must have the strength of will and the patience to endure the initial discomfort in order to achieve long-lasting success.

Let us return to our fictitious scenario to see how a counterintuitive move might play out.

Dr. Patella addresses the meeting: "I wonder if I might address everyone before we decide whether to adopt the changes recommended by Dr. B in the PowerPoint presentation?

We have implemented a number of changes to communication procedures in the past with the expectation that we can resolve our ongoing conflict and rather gloomy workplace environment. None of them seem to have had the desired effect in the long term. We just seem to fall back to the old ways.

Can I suggest that we try something different this time? Why don't we ask the interns, residents, and nurses working with the chief of staff to create their own solutions to the problems that we have in the unit? We can ask a mediator to help us organize a process for our discussions and that mediator can ensure that every group affected has a representative at the table. But the final solutions to conflict should be created by the interns, nurses, residents, and chief of staff working together.

We need to have a representative from residents, interns, nurses, *and* chief of staff all equally involved in creating and implementing change. Could we agree to adjourn our final decision on Dr. B's PowerPoint recommendations until the mediation is conducted and completed?"

Dr. B interrupts Dr. Patella: "Well, what is so important about this mediation? I have spent six weeks working on this PowerPoint presentation, and it's an exact replica of a very successful reorganization currently working in Toronto!"

Dr. Patella replies: "You may or may not be right about the potential success of the proposed reorganization, but our group of residents and nurses are not prepared to come onside until the meeting with a mediator happens. The group has identified a number of topics for discussion: broken promises, lack of team support from Dr.

Blood, micromanagement by Dr. Blood, lack of support for our group initiatives, and in some cases we are concerned about disrespect in Dr. Blood's interactions with both nursing and resident staff. The meeting with the mediator should help us focus and hopefully resolve all of these underlying conflicts. Then we can address your PowerPoint presentation!"

So, what has happened here? Dr. Patella has introduced a counterintuitive process. Instead of retaining and accepting the recommendations of an outside expert, Dr. Patella suggests that the core group (those with the real power to achieve long-lasting solutions), the residents, interns, nurses, *and* chief of staff meet, engage in a principled communication, and create their own solution to the problems facing the unit.

Of course, the meeting will have to be with a mediator. But we argue that the initial discomfort, initial stress of face-to-face probing of underlying issues, and the needs driving the conflict will give way to discovery and to brainstorming solutions for mutual gain.

In essence, the core group will be catalyzed to create and implement its own solutions to the conflict.

Talking Points

Mandated changes to the workplace are often unsuccessful in achieving lasting solutions to conflict or communication breakdown. We suggest that the core group must be catalyzed to create its own solutions to the problems through counterintuitive action followed by principled dialogue fostered in the course of mediation with a qualified mediator. ■

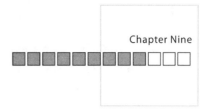

Chapter Nine

Identification of Issues and Interests

In this chapter, we explore the meaning of underlying interests and needs, the principled development of issues emanating from underlying interests, and the creation of the neutral agenda. We go on to examine the process of brainstorming options for mutual gain, the creation of the win-win, and the implementation of the win-win to achieve resolution of workplace conflict.

Many conflict-avoidance protocols in the workplace, both in healthcare and in the corporate world, have as their ultimate goal (and simultaneous failure), the avoidance of vulnerability, the avoidance of embarrassment, and the appearance of competence. Paradoxically, true and lasting resolution of conflict in the workplace may actually involve a process of actively seeking out conflict and proactively engaging in a principled protocol of communication to uncover the underlying needs and interests driving the conflict. We strongly recommend that solutions to workplace conflict be developed not by "top down" directions, memos, or directives but by the parties to the conflict, utilizing a five-step process called the Principled Negotiation Protocol.[56]

In order to view this principled negotiation protocol in action, let us return to ABC Hospital. A meeting has been convened to review a long list of complaints about operations in the Emergency Department. A facilitator, skilled in principled negotiation protocol, is present to chair the meeting.

Facilitator: "Good morning and welcome representatives from the hospital administration, doctors, nurse clinicians, and residents. We have three hours set aside this morning to engage in what I expect will be a successful and proactive dialogue. There is no preset agenda. We will create the agenda ourselves. We have only one goal: to develop a successful protocol for managing patient expectations in the Emergency Department of ABC Hospital.

In order to permit as much opportunity for exchange of ideas as possible, could we agree that everyone at the table will have an opportunity to make an uninterrupted opening statement to their present concerns with respect to our Emergency Department operations? After each party has had an opportunity to speak, I hope you will permit me to ask some questions to clarify issues that we need to talk about. Perhaps then we can work together to create an agenda for our meeting."

In many conflict scenarios, parties in conflict continue to focus on *positions*. Positions reflect the final desire or hoped-for solution of each party. They are generally not useful as tools of communication. Positions sound like this:

"I will not continue to work in this job for a dime less than $12,000 a month!"

or

"This is the final schedule for resident rotation. No changes can be accommodated."

or

"We will not tolerate continued disrespect for the value of our work. We want an immediate increase of $5.00 per hour for each hour of overtime."

Positions are the predominant points of contention. Parties in conflict are happy to repeat them, over and over. Positions entrench parties and act as barriers to conflict resolution. In order to begin dialogue to resolve conflict, we must identify the interests and needs *driving* the position. Once interests and needs are elicited, issues can be properly framed, meaningful agendas can be created, and parties can begin the process of determining options for solutions and options for mutual gain.

The process of uncovering interests through utilization of the tools of communication that we have reviewed in Chapter Four can be undertaken between the parties by direct communication with the assistance of a facilitator.

In order to examine the process of probing positions to uncover underlying interests, let us return to our meeting of the Emergency Department healthcare professions. Prior to the meeting the facilitator has asked each party to prepare a synopsis of the problems confronting Emergency Department communication from their perspective. The key to the process is uncovering the basic human needs (Maslow's Hierarchy of Needs): the hopes, fears, beliefs, and values underlying the stated positions. Interests may be consciously held or they may be deeply buried in the subconscious. These interests must be discovered if the parties in conflict are to move beyond stated positions to a dialogue that uncovers shared interests and needs and that bridges the gap between disparate interests and needs.

We will call these various synopses "opening positions" as they are each party's intended solution to the problem.

Al Blood, chief hospital administrator: "We are concerned about the intransigent attitude of staff in emergency, both nursing and residents. We have tried everything—meetings, directives, retreats, changes to the physical plant. Nothing seems to reduce the complaining and the constant negativity. We are of the view that staff really don't want to work collaboratively to improve waiting times, to address clinical issues, or to improve training. We feel there is no point in expending any further effort with the nurses or residents."

Facilitator: "So, do I understand that creating a collaborative working environment and maintaining positive morale amongst staff is important to administration?"

Al Blood: "Absolutely!"

Jane Doe, senior nurse clinician: "Well, I am delighted to hear that hospital administration is interested in staff collaboration. I haven't seen much evidence of that in the past. For three years we've been telling you that our emergency waiting times have escalated to unmanageable levels. We're here on the frontline day after day. Administration bombards us with directives and procedure protocols that we have had little or no impact in creating, and we have no time to implement! The triage area is like a war zone—angry patients blaming nurses for the lengthy delays, waiting endless hours for specialty consults, conflicts between the residents and other healthcare professions over patient care—leaving nursing staff caught in the middle. Burned-out senior nurses who are not pulling their weight and just marking time until retirement, leaving all the grunt work to other more junior staff to do. No one will assure us that it will get better instead of worse in the future! We want administration to implement the changes we have repeatedly suggested immediately."

Facilitator: "So, do I understand that your nurses feel 'left out of the loop' in relation to the decision-making processes that affect emergency services and that you want to work with administration and attending physicians to develop effective solutions to address patient waiting times, inter-professional conflict in the unit, and nursing morale?"

Jane Doe: "Yes, we want to change a number of clinical and operations protocols in a manner that really addresses the problems in communication and ongoing chronic conflict from the bottom up instead of top down. We need more power over our working environment and day-to-day operations."

Dr. Bone Marrow, senior staff physician: "Our group sees a complete breakdown in working relationships with nursing staff and administration. We can't get patients admitted to the wards in a timely manner. No one from administration has come up with a lasting solution to this vexing problem. Also, in our view, there is a constant conflict with nursing staff, many of whom are inexperienced in clinical procedures in triage or are senior nursing staff who won't follow our residents' orders and who constantly complain about everything, or worse, just leave for a coffee break whenever they feel like it. We are misleading the public when we represent that we can provide proper medical care in the Emergency Department of ABC Hospital. We can't. There isn't enough money, resources, or space for our physicians to deliver the medical attention they were trained to provide in medical school."

Facilitator: "So, do I understand that you want to work with hospital administration and the region to develop immediate and effective solutions to expedite patient flow through the Emergency Department, to change admissions procedures, and to improve the day-to-day working relationships between your physicians and nursing staff?"

Dr. Bone Marrow: "Yes. That's it in a nutshell!"

At this stage of the principled conflict-resolution protocol, the facilitator is endeavouring to elicit the needs/interests underlying the doctors' and nurses' positions and to reframe those needs and interests in a positive manner. The facilitator will, through a series of probing, clarifying, and open-ended questions, seek to identify neutral issues that all parties can agree upon, thus encouraging the parties to move forward to create their own agenda of items for discussion and potential resolution. The facilitator is moving the parties off their positions so they can engage in more productive problem solving.

The creation of the agenda in a principled interest-based negotiation is an entirely different process than is usually undertaken in a hierarchical organization. The key differences relate to the manner in which the agenda is created and the function of the agenda once it is created.

In the hierarchical organization, the agenda is created by one person or party. The wording of the agenda is chosen by that party. The agenda is created on a topical basis. Often the items for discussion are *positional*—with little attention given to underlying needs or interests of all parties affected by the topics. The hierarchical agenda is usually created in advance of a meeting and not easily subject to adjustment once the meeting has begun. Finally, the "solutions" to topics on the hierarchical agenda are driven by motives of expediency, cost effectiveness, "committee" recommendation, or simple fatigue. (In this last respect, think of the quality of attention given by attendees at most meetings to topic #15 in a four-page agenda!)

By contrast, in an interest-based negotiation process the existence of the agenda does not predate the meeting of the parties. Instead, the agenda is created by collaborative oral effort in which all parties have an equal say as to content, structure, and order. Further, the actual wording of the agenda reflects a level of communication in which the underlying interests and needs of all parties have been elicited to create disclosure of issues to be discussed. The wording used will be neutral.

The development of the neutral agenda provides an opportunity for the parties to develop a guideline or structure for their discussions. This assists the parties in shifting of positions and into an exploration of interest. Instead of focusing on positions they can look for options that will meet the interests of all the parties involved.

The way the issue is stated can have a significant impact on how the parties view the discussion or negotiation. It is important to frame the issues in joint neutral language that encourages joint problem solving. The issue should not suggest a solution, particularly if it is one party's solution. Because defining the issue can be difficult, it helps to think of the issue as the question that must be answered in order to reach resolution.

An agenda for the meeting of the ABC Hospital Emergency Department developed from the exploration of interests and re-framing of the facilitator may look like the agenda below.

Agenda

1. Develop a successful protocol for managing patient expectations in the Emergency Department of ABC Hospital.

2. Identify steps to create a more collaborative working environment in triage.

3. Examine patient flow through emergency in the past six months and identify problem areas.

4. Create and implement additional protocols to open up wards to receiving admitted patients from emergency.

5. Improve day-to-day working relationships between doctors and nurses.

As the parties move through the issues on the interest-based agenda, the facilitator will seek to identify their common and complimentary interests and will assist the parties to generate creative options for mutual gain of these interests. Where conflicting interests may exist, the facilitator will seek to focus the parties on developing objective standards to assess the efficacy of conflicting interests. The agenda becomes like a living creature: flexible, creative, and ultimately giving power to all interested parties to the conflict.

In the next chapter, we explore the collaborative processes that follow once common and conflicting interests have been identified from the agenda.

Talking Points

i) True and lasting resolution of conflict in the workplace may involve a process of actively seeking out conflict and proactively engaging in a principled protocol of communication (principled negotiation) to uncover the underlying needs and interests driving the conflict.

ii) Solutions to workplace conflict should be developed by the parties to the conflict utilizing a five-step process: the Principled Negotiation Protocol. In chronic conflict situations, it will often be necessary for parties to the conflict to retain a facilitator. The facilitator will work with the parties to collaboratively create an agenda of issues. The facilitator will assist the parties to uncover their interests and needs underlying the issues on the agenda and will assist the parties to identify common interests, complementary interests, and divergent interests. ■

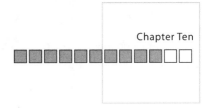

Chapter Ten

Building Bridges: Brainstorming Options for Mutual Gain[57]

In 1995, author and academic J. Resnick published a prescient article on the future course of standard conflict-resolution processes (trials, adjudicative court-oriented processes). In the context of his predictions of the growing popularity of out-of-court processes—mediation, principled negotiation, the collaborative dialogue—as mechanisms for resolving conflict, Resnick made the following prediction: "I believe we are approaching a time when many a civil trial will be described as a pathological event."[58]

Anyone who has ever been a party to a lawsuit, whether as a plaintiff or as a defendant, would probably concur that we are already there! Litigation as a primary means of resolving conflict is simply too expensive, too stressful, and too difficult to access or utilize as an efficient tool for the majority of people. Many individuals in conflict, whether acute or chronic, need cost-efficient, expeditious access to a process for final resolution that can be learned and applied successfully without the aid of expensive lawyers and third-party decision makers such as the courts, arbitrators, or tribunals.

Principled negotiation, as a concept and a relatively inexpensive process, has evolved in the last twenty-five years to fill this need. While the use of negotiation per se (as a means of back and forth communication designed to reach agreement between two or more parties with some shared interests and conflicting or different interests) dates back to pre-biblical times, the Harvard Negotiation Project and its researchers have refined and identified the structure of successful negotiation. Principled negotiation has been redefined to mean a collaborative process of engagement in dialogue and interaction that culminates in win-win for all parties to a conflict.

Bruce Patton, co-author of *Getting to Yes* and co-founder and deputy director of the Harvard Negotiation Project, identifies seven crucial elements inherent in the structure of all principled (win-win) negotiation processes:[59]

1. The identification of a party's interest (underlying needs, wants, motivations).

2. The achievement of a sense of fairness or legitimacy for the process and the resolution.

3. The creation and maintenance of a relationship with the parties both during and after the negotiation that is sufficient to permit the parties to continue a dialogue to the point of creating and implementing a win-win solution.

4. The extent to which the parties engage in a reasoned and critical analysis of what courses of action can realistically be taken in the event that one or both of the parties walk away from the negotiation (often described as assessment of the BATNA—best alternative to negotiated agreement).

5. The kind of communication that will occur between the parties as they engage in the negotiation:

- Adversarial

- Threatening

- Accommodating

- Compromising

6. The process of creating, considering, and evaluating options for solutions to the conflict.

7. The specifics of the commitment that will be sought and implemented in the process of achieving solutions to the conflict.

In this chapter, we seek to link the seven elements to the penultimate dialogue in the negotiation process: the parties' creation of options to be considered as win-win solutions for the conflict. We refer to this element of the negotiation process as "brainstorming options for mutual gain."

In order to examine this process as it might actually unfold in a conflict, let us examine a fictitious meeting involving a dispute over development of hospital discharge protocol in the case of elective surgery. The conflict has escalated as doctors, residents, and nurses meet with hospital administration in an attempt to create a new discharge protocol for elective surgery. Attendees at the meeting:

Dr. A	Chief of Surgery
Dr. B	Chief Surgery Resident
Nurse Z	Senior Nurse Clinician
Jane Doe, M.D., M.B.A.	Administrator of Hospital ABC
Dr. C	Board Representative
Ann Arbour	Mediator/Facilitator

The parties, working with a facilitator, have previously created an agenda and have worked diligently to examine common interests and needs amongst the various professionals—nurses, physicians, administrators, residents, and the region. After three hours, the facilitator has whiteboarded those common interests in the following manner:

1. An efficient elective-procedure discharge protocol (that will minimize time of unsuccessful nurse-physician communication such as calls to home of the resident or surgeon after hours, paging resident for clarification of doctor's discharge instructions).

2. A protocol that will clarify hospital expectations of nursing staff for handling patient calls to hospital after discharge.

3. A protocol that will establish a fast, accurate channel for urgent communication re: patient–nurse–resident–surgeon in connection with post-operative complications after discharge from hospital.

4. A protocol to address effective patient education re: post-surgical/post-discharge communication with the hospital.

We join the meeting as the facilitator addresses everyone:

Facilitator: "I just want to be certain that we now have a complete listing of all of your interests arising from the agenda that we jointly created in today's meeting. Does anyone have any item that we should add to the whiteboard?"

[A chorus of replies]

"Yes, I think you have captured the essence of what we need to incorporate in our elective surgery discharge protocol ..."

"I'm okay ..."

"That's accurate ..."

Facilitator: "All right then. I would like to take you to the next step in our dialogue in which everyone at the table has an opportunity to provide potential options or solutions to our whiteboard list of common interests. Before we begin, I wanted to take a moment to more fully explain the process at this stage of our dialogue. The key is to catalyze your creativity to get as many potential 'solutions' up on the whiteboard as possible to facilitate that conversation. I would ask you to first let the ideas flow freely, without pre-judgment, evaluation, criticism, or interruption.

I assure you that when this stage of our dialogue is finished, we will then work together to establish objective criteria to allow us to test and evaluate each potential solution—but that will come later, perhaps after lunch. For now, I encourage everyone to open up your creative thought processes. We will work rapidly and without interruption. If you will give me permission, I will write *all* of your ideas down on this whiteboard in no particular order or priority, just as you say them. If you agree, I suggest we let your ideas flow until the room goes quiet."

Bill Noonan, in "Managing Difficult Conversations,"[60] articulates the thought processes that are released during this stage of mutual learning and productive conversations. Noonan suggests that the key to engaging in productive conversations (i.e., those conversations that often result in creative solutions to conflict) is curiosity. Non-critical brainstorming of potential solutions to a conflict, suggests Noonan, catalyzes curiosity and productive thinking. Noonan lists five critical important thinking habits engendered by curiosity:

1. Assume that we have only partial knowledge [and by inference that others may have the knowledge we lack].

2. Grant legitimacy to the other perspectives in the dialogue.

3. Assume positive intentions on the part of others.

4. Acknowledge that our words and actions might have unintentional consequences—be open to learning and understanding how others are affected by our proposed solutions to conflict.

5. Embrace learning.

The process of brainstorming options for mutual gain creates the opportunity to engage in all of these thinking habits.

Let us return to our fictitious brainstorming session to observe the participants:

> Dr. A: "All right, I'll throw out the first idea ... PDAs for everyone—nurses, residents, staff."
>
> Dr. B: "Joint weekly stand-up only meetings with nurses, residents, and administration. No agenda, no seating, just talk!"
>
> Dr. Baker: "Nurses and surgery residents jointly write the new process."
>
> Nurse Z: "Hospital clarification of diagnostic responsibility of nursing staff in post-discharge patient communication with patients. Pay nurses for taking initiative to retrain and upgrade."
>
> Jane Doe: "Education—interactive video kiosks for patients to watch before their discharge from the hospital."

The key to successfully brainstorming options for mutual gain lies in the free flow of ideas, the non-evaluative, non-judgmental white-boarding of those ideas for all to observe, and the sense of empowerment for parties who engage in this form of dialogue. Brainstorming options for mutual gain requires participants to engage in what Professor Chris Argyris identifies as "double loop learning." Double loop learning depends on "questioning one's own assumption and behaviour," says Argyris.[61] The process of brainstorming, while temporarily suspending our evaluation and judgment of options for mutual gain, feeds into the most beneficial type of learning—to create solutions to conflict and to figure out our own role in the creation of the problem in the first place. Brainstorming removes the inhibition of defensive reasoning (the tendency to defend our role in conflict or threatening situations). The very process of being able to suggest solutions to conflict without being required to simultaneously defend our rationale or control the outcome opens up the dialogue, encourages reflection, and allows parties to challenge policies, practices, and actions without embarrassment or threat.

Argyris reasons that many forms of modern communication in large organizations create barriers to candour, forthrightness, commitment to learning, and self-empowerment. The step of encouraging employees and management to explore or brainstorm novel options to achieve win-win is rarely undertaken.

In many healthcare organizations there is, we suggest, an over-reliance on protocol, policy, systems, meetings, agendas, management guidelines, and hierarchy. Brainstorming works at a deeper level. It engenders an environment in which participants feel free to proactively question their own behaviour as well as the "behaviour" of the organization within without fear of adverse consequences. Properly utilized and practised, brainstorming options in a group setting facilitated by a neutral can achieve a new level of "self awareness, candour and responsibility."[62]

Talking Points

i) The key to finding solutions to conflict is the capacity to brainstorm options for mutual gain. Brainstorming allows parties to engage in the free flow of ideas and to suspend evaluation and judgment. Brainstorming removes the barrier of defensive reasoning and permits parties to suggest solutions without being required to simultaneously defend them.

ii) The key to engaging in productive conversations (i.e., those conversations that often result in creative solutions to conflict) is curiosity.

iii) In our experience, some situations in which brainstorming may work very well as a mechanism for productive ways to find solutions are:

- Where chronic conflict exists and the parties have failed to find a solution to the problem. Meeting together as a group, rather than working individually, to develop options creates new energy, which in turn results in a plethora of new ideas and solutions.

- In large organizations where problem solving may be overwhelming for individuals, brainstorming in groups can be very effective.

- In organizations or groups where power imbalances exist individuals may feel "safer," offering solutions and ideas in brainstorming sessions where everyone is encouraged to participate.

iv) Key considerations to setting up a brainstorming process are:

- To ensure a "supportive climate" (as described in Chapter Four) has been created where people feel safe in offering their ideas and feel their input is valued.

- To create an informal and comfortable setting where participants can relax.

- To have available a flip chart, whiteboard, or some other method for recording options that the whole group can view at once.

- To assign someone to record all options offered.

- To ask the participants to be as creative as possible when thinking of possible solutions for each issue identified.

- To remind everyone that there is no evaluating or judging when brainstorming and limit discussion of each option until brainstorming is exhausted.

- Once a number of options have been suggested the parties must work together to develop the options that look promising.

- Be careful not to curtail or stop brainstorming prematurely. ■

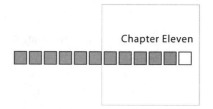

Chapter Eleven

Reaching Agreement: Evaluation and Implementation of Solutions

We now move into the final dialogue in the negotiation process. Once the parties have generated a substantial number of solutions through the brainstorming process described in Chapter Ten, assessment and evaluation of the proposed solutions commences. To attempt any evaluation of options before the parties have fully exhausted their ability to generate further options inhibits the brainstorming process and will result in a less comprehensive collection of options to evaluate for acceptability.

When we assess the proposed solutions for acceptability, it is important that the parties assess these options in terms of meeting all three elements of the Conflict Triangle discussed in Chapter Six. Remember that every conflict involves three elements: people, process, and problem. More specifically, every conflict involves a history of relationships and personalities amongst people and these people come with emotions. It also involves a process that refers to the pattern of interaction between the parties and the way it intensifies, eases, or spreads the conflict. Finally, all conflicts have content or substance—the issues and interests that are the reasons for the dispute. Any lasting resolution in a principled negotiation must recognize and address all three sides of the Conflict Triangle.[63]

Options are generally evaluated using the following criteria:

- Is it feasible?
- Does it address the parties' common interests?
- Is it fair? Does it satisfy objective criteria?
- Can it be implemented?

Thus the review will entail application of the above criteria to each of the proposed options.

Continuing on with our fictitious scenario in Chapter Ten, the facilitator is now ready to assist the parties in moving to agreement.

Facilitator: "We have generated a lot of ideas and it would seem for the time being that we have exhausted all the possibilities we can think of. It probably makes sense at this time to have a closer look at those options. In order to evaluate and assess the options, it is important to look at each of the proposed solutions and evaluate them in terms of meeting the substantive, emotional, and procedural needs of the group. This process will seem similar to what we did when we identified issues as we will once again review the interests of all of you to see how these solutions may meet those interests. You had identified the following common interests ...

Nurse Z, how do the proposed options of Personal Digital Assistants (PDAs) and weekly meetings meet the common interests we identified?"

Nurse Z: "Well, I don't think these PDAs are going to work really well because if the doctors or residents don't send discharge instructions we are in the same boat as before. I am also concerned that email messages may lead to confusion or misunderstanding. What if I need to clarify something with a doctor? I think that is better accomplished through verbal communication followed up with written clarification. I do like the option of weekly meetings. I think that might meet our need to minimize unsuccessful communication between doctors and nurses. I am not sure though that any of these help with the after-discharge care of patients."

Dr. B: "I think PDAs will work fine. We can email our discharge instructions and can also clarify instructions by email. If someone is still uncertain then I would be receptive to receiving calls at home. I just don't want unnecessary calls. I am not too keen on weekly meetings though. I already meet once a week with my residents group, twice a month with my program director, and I have a number of other meetings. It would be very difficult to schedule another weekly meeting. I think I speak for all of the residents when I say this."

Facilitator: "Does anyone have any suggestions on how we can meet the concerns raised by Nurse Z and Dr. B?"

Dr. A: "Well if we combine some of these options, such as supplying everyone with PDAs and training on how to use PDAs, institute monthly meetings to discuss nurse-doctor relationships, and develop a process as a group for patient discharge after elective surgery, I think we will have met all of our common interests. I am concerned with how we are going to implement all this. I am also concerned that we will not be able to address our interests that are not common. The members of my department have a lot of things they want, but someone has to pay for all this. I have a budget I have to stick to which administrators and I are accountable for. I may not have the resources to pay for this."

So, you can see from assessing the options in terms of needs and interests, the parties are able to work together to refine the options and at times dovetail some together to come up with a plan that may work for their department. Dr. A, however, raises two good questions:

- What do we do when there are interests that cannot be reconciled?

- How do you implement chosen solutions, especially if implementation requires involvement by a third party?

On occasion, parties are unable to arrive at solutions that can accommodate the interests of all parties. In those cases, Fisher, Ury, and Patton[64] recommend insisting on the use of objective criteria as a means of negotiating independent of each party's will. This turns the negotiation into a negotiation to find the appropriate standard, not a battle of wills. In developing objective criteria, the authors suggest it is important to ask two questions: how do you develop objective criteria, and how do you use them?

Fisher, Ury, and Patton suggest *(and we strongly recommend)* that objective criteria be free of the will of any of the parties and be legitimate and practical. They further suggest that it must apply to either party, i.e., reciprocal application.

Examples of objective criteria include:

- Market value

- Cost

- Equal treatment

- Precedent

- Industry practice

In the above scenario the parties may choose to look at the cost of implementing the various options, and they may also rely on precedent established in other departments or hospitals.

In addition to using objective criteria you must apply a process of fair procedure. More specifically, you can pick a process for deciding, i.e., taking turns, letting someone else decide, trying something for a while, and then trying something else. Another possibility suggested by Fisher, Ury, and Patton in *Getting to Yes* [65] is to "fractionate" the problems into smaller, more manageable problems and look for partial *verbal* agreements or temporary verbal agreements that can eventually be developed (if necessary) into written protocol, i.e., Can you try to use PDAs for the next three months and see how that goes? Most people can commit to something for a short term. In terms of the ABC Hospital scenario above, this may mean reaching a short-term agreement that the doctors and nurses will communicate discharge instructions by PDA and an agreement on designating a committee of doctors, nurses, and residents to prepare a draft protocol for review. By agreeing to two smaller issues and successfully implementing these they will build momentum for further agreement on the tougher issues.

Once the parties confirm that common interests can be met by the proposed solutions and that the conflicting interests can also be met through the application of objective criteria or fair procedure, the parties will need to carefully assess and detail how the proposed solutions will be implemented. This may involve the following steps:

- Establish a plan for implementing the option chosen— How? When? What?

- Identify the people who have the power to implement the agreement.

- Consider a follow-up plan for ensuring agreements are implemented.

- Consider who needs to be informed and included in the plan.

- Consider how disputes arising through implementation will be addressed.

- Track changes over time.

In order to formalize the agreement reached, it is important to have some sort of process for confirming the parties' commitment, such as a verbal agreement witnessed by other parties, a written memorandum of understanding signed by the parties, or a full-out legal contract.

In our scenario of creating a discharge process for patients, the agreements reached should be formalized in writing probably through a memorandum of understanding or a written protocol. The memorandum of understanding will outline in detail the agreement reached, the steps necessary to implement the agreement, the parties that need to be involved, the method for reviewing the efficacy of the newly developed protocol, and a process or procedure for addressing any necessary changes to the protocol. A memorandum of understanding may look like the memorandum set out below:

Memorandum of Understanding

Dr. A, Dr. B, Nurse Z, Ms. Jane Doe, and Dr. C have agreed to the following with respect to developing a hospital discharge process for elective surgery:

Terms:

1. All doctors, nurses, and residents within this department will be provided with PDAs within one month so that they can communicate discharge instructions with each other. In the event discharge instructions cannot be communicated by PDA the discharging doctor or resident may be contacted at home or at the office.

2. The use of the PDA will be reviewed by the parties within three months of the PDAs being distributed.

3. The doctors, nurses, and residents of this department will have monthly meetings where they will

discuss ongoing issues relating to the new discharge processes and other patient care issues. All doctors, residents, and nurses must be present at these meetings unless specifically excused by Dr. A.

4. Training and education opportunities will be made available to nursing staff who wish to update or further their skills.

5. The nursing staff will appoint one nurse, the residents will appoint one resident, and the doctors will appoint one or two of their numbers to form a committee to develop hospital discharge processes for elective surgery. The committee will meet on a weekly basis for the next six weeks in order that they may develop a draft process to bring back to the group for further facilitated discussion. As part of this process, this committee will explore the possibility of developing written materials and video presentations for patients to review prior to discharge.

6. Dr. A will develop a budget for PDAs, prepare discharge materials and re-training, and present the same to administration for approval within four weeks of this meeting.

7. If there are any problems encountered in implementing any part of this agreement, the parties will meet with a facilitator again to try to resolve those identified problems or concerns.

Dated _____   Nurse Z _____

Dr. A _____   Jane Doe _____

Dr. B _____

Dr. C _____

Talking Points

i) Once the parties have generated a substantial number of solutions through the brainstorming process, assessment and
evaluation of the proposed solution commences. Options are
generally evaluated using the following criteria:

- Is it feasible?

- Does it address the parties' common interests?

- Is it fair? Does it satisfy objective criteria of fairness?

- Can it be implemented?

ii) On occasion, parties are unable to arrive at solutions that can
accommodate the interests of all. In those cases, Fisher, Ury,
and Patton recommend insisting on the use of objective criteria as a means of negotiating independent of each party's will.[66]
Fair procedure can be applied, i.e., taking turns, letting someone else decide, trying something for a while and then trying
something else. Another possibility is to "fractionate" the
problems into smaller, more manageable problems and to
look for partial agreements or temporary agreements that can
eventually be developed into full agreements.

iii) The parties need to carefully assess and detail how the proposed solutions will be implemented. In order to formalize the
agreement reached, it is important to have some sort of process
for confirming each party's commitment, such as a verbal
agreement witnessed by other parties, a written memorandum
of understanding signed by the parties, or a legal contract. ■

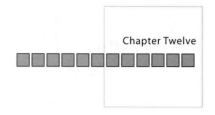

Chapter Twelve

The Apology

One of the most difficult aspects of dialogue and of principled negotiation is the apology. There will be many occasions in the workplace in which conflict simply cannot be resolved until an apology is made. Apology in the context of healthcare is often exceptionally difficult, especially where the standard of care is the issue or where patient harm has occurred. Readers of this chapter would be well advised to consult their respective professional bodies in the context of making apologies to patients. Our focus is directed toward the issue of apology as it affects healthcare professionals *inter se* and in their patient interactions.

In his *locus classicus* text, *On Apology*, Aaron Lazare defines apology in the following elegant manner:

> Apology is best understood not as what one party (the offender) offers to another party (the offended) but as a process in which both parties reach an agreement through "give and take" as a way to deal with the initial problem.[67]

Lazare lists all of the aspects of apology that can be the subject of negotiation:

1. The degree of responsibility that each party will accept.

2. The quantum of remorse that must be expressed.

3. The timing of the apology.

4. The amount of venting to be expressed by each party.

5. The type of reparation to be offered and accepted.

Lazare suggests that true apology involves a bilateral healing process ending in "win-win" for both the offender and offended in the sense that the relationship is restored and healed for the future. Rendering a true apology is hard work. Why do we find it so difficult to apologize? All too often our words are generalized and uttered in haste. The result? In many cases, permanent damage to the working relationship and, in some cases, destruction of the very structure of the entire environment with a profound impact on third parties, namely patients and co-workers.

To examine the elements of a negotiated apology between healthcare professionals, we review two fictitious scenarios:

Dr. Cell: chief of surgery

Dr. Zed: senior resident assisting Dr. Cell in surgery—comminuted fracture

Both doctors have just exited the operating theatre where they have performed surgical repair of comminuted fractures of the tibia and fibula. A fifteen-minute delay arose during surgery where one of the surgical instruments was unaccounted for at the conclusion of the procedure. Dr. Cell blew up at Dr. Zed in front of the junior residents and operating room nurses. Profanity was used. Dr. Cell blamed Dr. Zed and called him a "blithering idiot." Moments later they discovered there had been a miscount of instruments. It had nothing to do with Dr. Zed's performance.

First let us review Dr. Cell's inner thoughts as he exits the operating theatre.

"Darn! I've done it again! Lost my temper! Blown up at my best resident. I've embarrassed him in front of everyone in the operating theatre. I was just so concerned we'd lost an instrument in the patient. He was so obese! I don't need the aggravation of another patient complaint or adverse incident. I need a holiday! Why do I take out my frustrations on others without forethought? What is the matter with me?"

Dr. Cell to Dr. Zed (as they walk down to the shower and change): "Hey look, Bill. Sorry I blew up at you. Nothing personal. I just have too much stress right now! Next time, stand up for yourself when I lose my temper for no reason, especially when you know it's not your fault! [laughter]

Dr. Zed: "Oh yeah, sure!" (turning away to walk down another hall—any hall—just to get away)

Has an apology been given? Has any apology been accepted? Let us examine the words of the two parties from the protocol recommended by Aaron Lazare:

First:

Has Dr. Cell accepted any responsibility for his actions? We would suggest not. Dr. Cell utters the word "sorry" with a caveat: it wasn't meant to be a personal attack, other events in his personal life caused him to lose his temper. Even worse, Dr. Cell blames Dr. Zed for failing to "stand up" for himself to rebut the unjust criticism.

Second:

Has Dr. Cell communicated any *true remorse?* Again, we would suggest not. Even though Dr. Cell has used the word "sorry," he has compromised its healing effect by attributing his loss of temper to outside forces beyond his personal control.

Third:

Has Dr. Cell given any opportunity to Dr. Zed to communicate how the loss of temper, the profanity, and the name calling has affected him? Is there any bilateral dialogue? Again, the answer to this question is no. Dr. Zed has been given no opportunity to say *how* Dr. Cell's loss of temper, name calling, belittling—all taking place in front of other healthcare professionals—has affected him.

Finally:

Have the words uttered by Dr. Cell resulted in a healing of the bonds of the working relationship, allowing the parties to move forward? Probably not. There will likely be a continued undercurrent of resentment on the part of Dr. Zed and, even worse, no foreseeable change in the behaviour of Dr. Cell toward his subordinates in future interactions in the operating room.

In the second fictitious scenario, we examine an apology occurring between Dr. A, the attending physician, and her senior resident, Dr. B. The apology dialogue takes place at a restaurant across the street from the hospital. Dr. A has invited Dr. B to share soup/salad and dessert (her treat). We join the lunch as invisible observers just as Dr. A and Dr. B reach dessert.

Dr. A: "You know, Dr. B, I am glad you had time for lunch off-site today. I wanted to tell you how sorry I am for criticizing your charting protocol on grand rounds the day before yesterday in the manner that I did. I was wrong to use that sarcastic tone of voice. My choice of words was unwarranted and unprofessional. There is no excuse for losing my temper as I did. I have been so troubled by my loss of control. I have lost many hours of sleep since it happened—"

Dr. B (interrupting): "Don't worry! I know you don't usually conduct grand rounds that way. That was a difficult patient. We almost had an adverse event with his medication as a result of the charting error on the meds. My supervision of the junior resident should have been handled more closely. We had a close call. I'm just glad we caught it in time! I know we will have to report it, of course, to the Quality Assurance Committee."

Dr. A: "That is pretty decent of you, Dr. B. If you want I will circulate an email to our department confirming my apology to you. I will speak to the junior resident, who actually made the error in the patient's prescription, privately about some intensive refreshers in charting procedures. I will offer to be his mentor to ensure this type of error does not recur."

Dr. B: "Thanks, Dr. A. I really appreciate the time and effort you took to meet with me. I accept your offer to make amends without reservation!"

How does the apology compare with the first scenario? Again, we examine the dialogue from the perspective of Aaron Lazare's protocol:

First:

Has Dr. A accepted personal responsibility for her actions? We would suggest yes. The words "I am sorry," "I was wrong," and "there is no excuse" are all phrases of assumption of personal responsibility—with no caveats attached to minimize their effect.

Second:

Has Dr. A communicated true remorse for her words? The answer would appear to be yes based on the comment, "I have been so troubled by my loss of control, I have lost many hours of sleep."

Third:

Has an opportunity been given to Dr. B to convey how the unjust criticism affected him? Dr. B has had a full opportunity to tell Dr. A how he feels, how he was affected by her words. Dr. B has also conveyed to Dr. A that the quality of her expressed apology is sufficient for him. There is a sense of absolution given to Dr. A in the words of Dr. B: "I know you don't usually conduct grand rounds that way."

Finally:

Has reparation been offered and accepted? Dr. A has offered to confirm her apology to Dr. B via email to other members of the department. In other words, the apology will receive the same notoriety and publication as the original unjust criticism of Dr. B.

In summary, what are the essential elements of the effective apology?

1. Immediacy to the event giving rise to the apology.

2. Words expressing true remorse by the wrongdoer.

3. Words accepting responsibility with no caveat of condition.

4. An offer of reparation.

Summarized by the acronym:

Immediate

Remorse

Responsibility

Reparation

Anything less is *not* a true apology and will not heal the relationship.

The principles with respect to apology have even more significance when they involve interactions with families who express concerns about patient care, and equally in the situation of adverse events. ■

Dialogue and Apology
in the Context of Adverse Events

"The complexity of care in hospitals [in the twenty-first century] mandates that patients may receive care from several different [healthcare] providers, which [may] increase the risk of AE's [adverse events] [arising] from miscommunication and [issues of] coordination of care ... Efforts to make patient care safer will require leadership to encourage the reporting of adverse events, continued monitoring of the incidence of these events, the judicious application of new technologies and *improved communication and coordination among caregivers*"[68] [emphasis added] of communication protocols within the hospital at all levels, both human and technological.

The communication skill of healthcare providers is never more important than when patient harm has occurred. When patient harm occurs the healthcare workers have a responsibility to review what caused the harm, make changes and recommendations as necessary, and disclose these recommendations to the patient and/or the patient's family as the case may be.

The Health Quarterly Council of Alberta, in its published "Framework for Disclosure of Harm to Patients and Families" (July 2006), mandates that "disclosure of harm is the right thing to do." The provincial guidelines suggest that the actual content of the meeting between healthcare professionals and the patient honour the following guiding principles:

1. Respect for patient autonomy.

2. Meeting patient expectations.

3. Early acknowledgement of harm done.

4. A protocol for disclosure of relevant facts leading to the patient's current status.

5.   An immediate expression of regret to the patient and family.

The provincial guidelines mandate that only "facts related to the patient's diagnostic treatment and care information" (as defined by the Health Information Act section 1(1)(k)) should be shared:

- what happened

- the chronology

- test results

- consequences of the harm

- the changes to the treatment plan

- the changes to the system

Alberta legislation precludes disclosing information that could reasonably lead to the identification of a person who provided the health information in confidence (Health Information Act section 11(1)(b)), results of an investigation relating to a health service provider (Health Information Act section 11(2)(b)), or records of the Quality Assurance Committee and subcommittees conducting investigations.

The Health Quality Council of Alberta mandates two different protocols for disclosure of adverse events, dependent on whether the standard of care was met or not met:[69]

A. Where the standard of care was met, five steps are to be taken in meeting with the patient and family:

Step 1:   Begin with a "benevolent expression of regret."

Step 2:   Listen to the patient.

Step 3:   Express empathy.

-paraphrase and summarize through active listening

Step 4:   Apologize for the situation.

Step 5:   Explain what happened (secure first the permission of the patient before proceeding with explanations).

B. Where the standard of care was not met:

In situations of adverse event where it is determined that the standard of care was not met, the provincial policy mandates the following four-step T.E.A.M. approach developed by the U.S. Institute for Healthcare Communication, 2003:

Step 1: Truth

-state the facts, the chronology of events

Step 2: Empathize with the *experience* of the patient and family.

Step 3: Apologize

-take responsibility for what happened

-be accountable for taking steps to prevent similar situations in the future

Step 4: Manage all aspects of patient care to help in patient recovery.

In addition to the Provincial Disclosure Guidelines, the Canadian Patient Safety Institute has published a protocol for Disclosure of Adverse Events.[70] This particular protocol was developed with the input of a broad spectrum of interested parties including the Federation of Medical Regulatory Authorities, Canada, the Canadian Medical Protective Association, the Health Quality Council of Alberta, the Canadian Council of Health Services Accreditation, and the Canadian Patient Safety Institute.

The Disclosure Guidelines should be mandatory reading for all healthcare providers as they contain essential explanations of the stages of disclosure of adverse events, emphasize the importance of apology in the process, and provide a comprehensive protocol of what to disclose in the dialogue between the healthcare provider and patient. Perhaps the most important portion of the protocol is contained at page twenty-three, as it is in this section that "expression of regret" is defined, discussed, and emphasized:

> An early expression of regret that communicates genuine concern and sympathy for a patient's physical and emotional well-being is valuable and essential ...There is a belief that apology implies blame for providers which is often inconsistent with a just patient safety culture ... An apology to patients by healthcare providers or organizations should not be taken as an admission of legal responsibility.[71]

The foregoing complex guidelines highlight an interesting phenomenon that has developed in the past two decades in connection with apologies in healthcare. In the United States, thirty state legislatures have promulgated (proclaim or declare something officially) apology legislation. The express statutory aim of the legislation is to prohibit introduction of apologies in court as evidence of negligence in cases of medical malpractice. The expectation of legislators is that healthcare professionals who cause emotional and/or physical harm to their patients through inadvertence, error in judgment, and negligence will be encouraged by this statutory protection to extend expressions of apology without fear that such conversations will be introduced as evidence of an admission of negligence if subsequent litigation is commenced.

In Canada, apology legislation has been enacted in British Columbia and Saskatchewan. Legislation is pending in Manitoba and Yukon.[72] The British Columbian legislation was specifically enacted to negate the perceived concern that saying "I am sorry" will be equalled with "I am liable" or "I am negligent" or some other adverse legal consequence.

In addition to public policy arguments, proponents of apology legislation argue that an increase in physician/healthcare professional apology to patients will directly cause a decrease in medical malpractice litigation. The prevailing view is that true apology calms angry patients, assuages pain, and reduces their ill-will and desire to sue.

Talking Points

i) In general, the essential elements of the effective apology between healthcare providers are:

- Immediacy to the event giving rise to the apology

- Words expressing true remorse by the wrongdoer

- Words accepting responsibility with no caveat or condition

- An offer of reparation

ii) The communication skill of healthcare providers is never more important than when patient harm has occurred. The actual content of the meeting between the healthcare professional and the patient should honour the following guiding principles:

- Respect for patient autonomy

- Meeting patient expectations

- Early acknowledgement of harm done

- A protocol for disclosure of relevant facts leading to the patient's current status

- An immediate expression of regret to the patient and family. ■

Future Issues for Principled Communicators: Technology Barriers

O n March 11, 2008, the *Calgary Herald* published a fascinating article in the Business Section authored by Jessica Guynn, a reporter for the *Los Angeles Times*. The reporter disclosed an interesting trend in the birthplace of technology, Silicon Valley. More and more companies are banning laptops, Blackberries, iPhones, and other personal communication devices from business meetings. Why? Listen to what Todd Wilkens of the San Francisco design firm Adaptive Path wrote in his company blog in November 2007 (as reproduced in Guynn's report):

> In this age of wireless internet and mobile e-mail devices, having an effective meeting or working session is becoming more and more difficult. Laptops, Blackberries, Sidekicks, iPhones and the like keep people from being fully present ... Aside from just being rude, partial attention generally leads to partial results.

The last phrase is so important for the future of communication in healthcare that it bears repeating. *Partial attention generally leads to partial results.*

As Guynn notes, "The ever increasing speed and power of technology allows employees to effortlessly toggle back and forth between tasks. The wireless revolution has only accelerated this trend, turning every laptop computer into a lightning-quick mobile communication hub."

Guynn has support from academia for her conclusion that technology may in fact be *impeding* communication in the workplace. Her article refers to studies undertaken at Stanford University by Professor Pamela Hinds, who studies the effects of technology on groups. Professor Hinds is quoted in Guynn's article with the following cogent observation on a potentially alarming trend in communication:

> It's increasingly difficult to get people's undivided attention ... people would argue that they are attending to the most important information without any loss of participation, but in fact they aren't fully there.

One has only to look at a university class in session with row upon row of students sitting behind the screens of their respective laptops—with no eye contact or personal interaction with the professor—to see actual confirmation of her rather worrisome observations. We are so engaged with our technological devices that we risk becoming *disengaged* with each other.

We look at the examples all around us for confirmation of this:

- Groups of twenty-somethings walking down the street together—all simultaneously texting or talking on their cell phones—ignoring the possibility of live communication with each other.

- Important meetings constantly interrupted by ringing cell phones—or worse, by fellow attendees who actually take these calls in the midst of, and in preference to, their face-to-face interaction with those who are physically present at the meeting. The excuse offered always is "I've got to take this call ..."

- Individuals who live online, who seek out virtual worlds, and who seem to prefer interaction and communication with an avatar rather than another human being.

Martin Cooper, the inventor of the cell phone in 1973, envisioned a world with people so connected to wireless that the devices would become embedded in their bodies.

In an article authored by Sinead Carew, Reuters, New York (reproduced in the *Calgary Herald,* March 30, 2008), Cooper predicts that:

> In about 15 to 20 years ... people [will] have embedded wireless devices in their bodies to help diagnose and cure illness. Just think of what a world it would be if we could measure the characteristics of your body when you get sick and transmit those directly to a doctor or a computer ... you could get diagnosed and cured instantly and wirelessly.

In an article by Claudine Beaumont, a reporter with London's *Telegraph* (reprinted in the *Calgary Herald),* there is an amazing prediction from Tim Berners-Lee, the man credited with inventing the World Wide Web. Beaumont reports that Berners-Lee envisions an internet in which "all information, applications and data are seamlessly linked and interwoven—everything will work with everything else and that will, in effect, allow us to live our lives almost entirely online." In Beaumont's article, she reports that Berners-Lee calls this new phenomenon "the Semantic Web," defined to be a state where "computers will understand the context of information and will be able to identify and *appreciate* [emphasis added] the complex links between people, places and data, pulling it together to deliver rich search results and a better online experience."

All of these predictions would seem to accept, without question, that future developments in technology, in the internet, and in the virtual world will improve the way in which we communicate with our environment and with each other.

But, we ask, what is the ultimate measuring stick for this bold prediction for the future efficacy of human communication?

Will the computer chips embedded in our bodies catch the nuance of an arched eyebrow? Will the Semantic Web help healthcare professionals to create and maintain a workplace that recognizes personal and professional worth, that creates a sense of value attached to one's job and association with the hospital or the clinic or even the patient?

In the year 2050, will a "warm" computer somewhere create a virtual world that expresses friendliness and fosters a sense of community such that workers within the workplace feel valued, respected, and recognized for their contributions?

Only time will tell. ■

Notes

Chapter One

1. Y. Donchin et al, "A Look into the Nature and Causes of Human Errors in the Intensive Care Unit," *Critical Care Medicine* 23, 2 (1995): 294–300; Wilson et al, "The Quality in Australian Health Care Study," *Medical Journal of Australia* 163, 9 (1995): 458–71; Bhasal et al, "Analysing Harm in Australian General Practice: An Incident Monitoring Study," *Medical Journal of Australia* 169 (1998): 173–76.

2. Rosemary Spencer and Pamela Logan, "Role-based Communication Problems within an Emergency Department Setting," (Centre for Health Informatics, University of New South Wales HIC), 2002.

3. H.B. Beckman and R.M. Frankel, "The Effect of Physician Behaviour on the Collection of Data," *Annuals of Internal Medicine* 101 (1984): 692–96.

4. Jorges Carreras, M.D., F.A.C.E.P., "Physicians with Good Communication Skills Are Made, Not Born," *NC Medical Journal* 54, 12 (1993): 652–53.

5. Lynne M. Kirk, M.D., and Linda Blank, "Professional Behavior—A Learner's Permit for Licensure," *The New England Journal of Medicine* 353, 25 (22 December 2005): 2709–2711.

6. William Isaacs, *Dialogue and the Art of Thinking Together* (New York: Doubleday, 1999), p. 47.

7. Isaacs, *Dialogue and the Art of Thinking Together.*

8. Ibid, p. 47.

9. For the purpose of our analysis, we have defined *chronic conflict* to mean an ongoing unresolved struggle involving interdependent parties arising from real or perceived differences in physical needs, security and safety needs, social needs, ego needs, or self-fulfillment needs. By contrast, *acute conflict* will be defined to include a sudden breakdown in the sending and receiving of accurate communication between or among persons who may or may not be involved in an ongoing interdependent relationship.

10. A.H. Maslow, "A Theory of Human Motivation," *Psychological Review* 50 (1943): 370–96.

Chapter Two

11. Professor Lila Love, visiting professor, Pepperdine Law School, Straus Institute, excerpt from Professor Love's course material and lecture, "Introduction to Mediation."

12. Ibid.

13. Ibid.

14. Roger Fisher and William Ury with Bruce Patton (editor), *Getting to Yes: Negotiating Agreement Without Giving In* (Boston: Houghton Mifflin, 1981).

15. *Needs* in this context is viewed from the perspective of Maslow's Hierarchy of Needs discussed in Chapter Three.

16. BATNA. The best alternative to negotiated agreement is unique to each conflict. The determination of BATNA is based upon the parties' assessment of the next-best course of action to take to achieve a solution to the conflict if no agreement is reached. In assessing the efficacy of BATNA, parties will examine costs, time, and the ability to achieve satisfaction of the underlying needs. The trick to BATNA is that it can act as a reality check as parties often come to the conclusion that they have no realistic BATNA! This realization serves as a catalyst to spur the parties on to attempt to achieve agreement.

17. There are five primary sources of confidentiality in mediation: rules of evidence, legal privileges, confidentiality statutes, mediation agreements, and positive disclosure obligations. Readers of this book would be well advised to review the excellent text, *Mediation: The Roles of Advocate and Neutral* by Dwight Golann and Jay Folberg (New York: Aspen Publishers, 2006), pp. 345–65. Fortunately, the mediator will guide the parties through confidentiality and disclosure issues. The mediator will ensure that a proper and executed confidentiality agreement is prepared with input from the parties. Indeed, the preparation of confidentiality agreements and rules of disclosure is one of the key functions of the mediator. Generally, confidentiality agreements deal with protection of information created in the course of mediation and prohibit the parties from disclosing the same in ongoing or subsequent litigation. Confidentiality agreements also prohibit the parties from issuing subpoenas to the mediator, thus protecting the mediator from being called to testify as to events that transpired in the mediation. The public policy aim of such agreements is to encourage candour and truth in the course of mediation.

Chapter Three

18. All fact patterns and all names of healthcare professionals presented in this book are entirely fictitious and are based on an amalgam of common issues and problems in the healthcare environment. Any resemblance to real people or real issues is entirely coincidental and unintended (The authors – Heather Lamoureux and Elaine Seifert).

19. Thomas Crum, *The Magic of Conflict: Turning a Life of Work into a Work of Art* (New York: Simon & Schuster Inc., 1987), p. 49.

20. M.L. DeFleur, *Theories of Mass Communication*, 1st ed. (New York: David Mckay Co., 1966).

21. Jessica Galante, unpublished thesis, Georgetown University Law Center.

22. A.H. Maslow, "A Theory of Human Motivation," 394–95.

23. Kenneth W. Thomas and Ralph W. Kilmann, *The Thomas-Kilmann Conflict Mode Instrument* (Tuxedo, NY: Xicom, 1974).

24. Kenneth W. Thomas, *Introduction to Conflict Management: Improving Performance Using the TKI* (Palo Alto, CA: CPP, 2002). Thomas is a professor of Administrative Sciences with extensive publications on conflict management. He has published in *Behavioural Science, Journal of Conflict Resolution,* and other professional journals. He received his Ph.D. from Purdue University in 1971.

Chapter Four

25. Dean Pruitt, Jeffery Rubin, and Sung Hee Kim, *Social Conflict: Escalation, Stalemate and Settlement,* 2nd ed. (New York: McGraw-Hill Inc., 1994), p. 69.

26. Ibid, p. 70.

27. Ibid, pp. 69–71.

28. Ibid, pp. 72–81. The summary of "content escalation" on pages 37 to 38 is based on the work of Pruitt, Rubin, and Kim.

29. Elaine Seifert, Q.C. and Sheila Newel, *The Right Team, The Right Approach, The Right Awareness, The Right Solution,* unpublished Leadership Training Manual (TriOcean Engineering, 2005).

30. Joseph P. Folger, Marshall Scott Poole, and Randall K. Stuntman, *Working through Conflict: Strategies for Relationships, Groups and Organizations,* 4th ed. (New York: Addison, Wesley, Longman, Inc., 2001), p. 185.

31. Jack Gibb, "Defensive Communication," *Journal of Communication* 2 (1961): 141–48.

32. Folger et al, *Working through Conflict,* pp. 217–18.

Chapter Five

33. Jerome Groopman, M.D., *How Doctors Think* (Boston: Houghton Mifflin Company, 2007).

34. Ibid, pp. 151–53 "... the utility of a certain outcome is multiplied by its probability."

35. Ibid, p. 153.

36. "Guide Book for Managing Disruptive Physician Behaviour," (Toronto: College of Physicians and Surgeons of Ontario), April 2008.

37. Health Maintenance Organization (HMO) is a specific type of healthcare plan found in the United States. See www.hmopage.org.

38. William Isaacs, "Taking Flight—Dialogue, Collective Thinking and Organizational Learning," *Elvesier Science Publishing Company Inc. Organizational* 2 (Autumn 1993): 27–39.

Chapter Six

39. D.D. Cahn, *Conflict in Intimate Relationships* (New York: Guilford, 1992).

40. Fisher, Ury, and Patton, *Getting to Yes,* p. 60

41. David A. Binder, Paul Bergman, and Susan C. Price, *Lawyers as Counsellors: A Client-Centered Approach*, 2nd ed. (St. Paul, MN: West Group Publishing, 2004).

42. Seifert and Newel, *The Right Team, The Right Approach, The Right Awareness, The Right Solution.*

43. The authors define destructive communication as communication that is not conducive to a principled communication. It may include such blatant things as criticizing, name calling, threatening, or intimidating but also more benign things such as arguing, interrupting, telling others what to do, or excessive questioning.

44. *Oxford Dictionary* definition: "Of or pertaining to Sigmund Freud, Austrian specialist in neurology and founder of psychoanalysis, or his teaching ..."

45. Michael Fogel, "Managing Successful Settlement Conferences," presentation at National Judicial Institute, November, 2001.

46. Ibid, Anger Management Model reproduced by Michael Fogel.

47. Steven Johnson, *Mind Wide Open: Your Brain and the Neuroscience of Everyday Life* (New York: Scribner, 2004), pp. 152–57.

48. Bill Noonan, "Managing Difficult Conversations," *The Learning Circle* (Boston: Harvard Business School Publishing Corporation, 2003). Dr. Noonan is an educator and expert in the Fifth Discipline Area of Mental Modes and has worked closely with Peter Senge on several e-learning and internet projects, including the multimedia CD ROM, *Activating the Fifth Discipline.*

49. Elaine Seifert, Q.C., and Laurie McMurchie, Q.C., "Moving from Theory to Practice: Practical Approaches to Family Law Negotiations" (Legal Education Society of Alberta, 2005).

50. Douglas Stone, Bruce Patton, and Sheila Heen, *Difficult Conversations* (Toronto: Penguin Books, 1999), p. 42.

51. Fisher, Ury, and Patton, *Getting to Yes,* p. 71.

52. We wish to thank mediator, lawyer, and educator Michael Fogel of Vancouver, British Columbia, for his incisive, thoughtful summary of processes to allow parties in conflict to begin to engage in dialogue.

53. Stone, Patton, and Heen, *Difficult Conversations,* p. 48.

Chapter Eight

54. Art Kleiner, *Who Really Matters: The Core Group Theory of Power, Privilege and Success* (New York: Doubleday, 2003)

55. For further reading on this topic we recommend Professor Peter Kollock's detailed study on cooperation, "Social Dilemmas: The Anatomy of Cooperation," *Annual Review of Sociology* 24 (1998): 183–214.

Chapter Nine

56. The five steps to the Principled Negotiation Protocol are summarized in Chapter Two. "In the name of positive thinking [healthcare professionals involved in administration/management/clinical training] often censor [or predetermine] what everyone needs to say and hear. [In so doing], managers deprive employees of the opportunity to take responsibility for their own behaviour by learning to understand it. The solu-

tion for this problem is 'double-loop learning,' which depends on questioning one's own assumptions and behaviour and the inherent value of the assumptions governing the protocol for conflict resolution in the workplace. Failing to use double-loop learning leads to selective data gathering and postulation of solutions that *do not* threaten the workplace culture and sloppy self-serving solutions which are a parody of a scientific method." Chris Argyris, "Good Communication That Blocks Learning," *Harvard Business Review* (July/August 1994): 77–85. Argyris is a professor at Harvard University.

Chapter Ten

57. These terms were first used extensively in the seminal text on conflict resolution *Getting to Yes* by Roger Fisher, William Ury, and Bruce Patton mentioned above.

58. J. Resick, "Many Doors? Closing Doors? Alternative Dispute Resolution and Adjudication," *Ohio State Journal of Dispute Resolution* 10 (1995): 261.

59. Bruce Patton, "Negotiation Power," *Executive Excellence* 18 (April 2001): 8.

60. Bill Noonan and Peter Senge in *Managing Difficult Conversations,* Interactive CD-ROM (Boston: Harvard Business School Publishing Corporation, 2003).

61. Chris Argyris, "Good Communication that Blocks Learning," p. 79.

62. Ibid, p. 85.

Chapter Eleven

63. Jennifer Stief and Eileen Beers, *Mediator's Handbook,* 3rd ed. (Gabriola Island, BC: New Society Publishers, 1998).

64. Fisher. Ury, and Patton, *Getting to Yes*, p. 69.

65. Ibid, p. 70.

66. Ibid.

Chapter Twelve

67. Aaron Lazare, *On Apology* (New York: Oxford University Press, 2004), p. 205.

68. "The Canadian Adverse Events Study: the incidence of adverse events among hospital patients in Canada," *CMAJ* 170, 11 (May 25, 2004): 1678–1686. *Words in square brackets are those of the authors.

69. *Disclosure of Harm to Patients and Families* (Health Quality Council of Alberta, July 2006).

70. *Canadian Disclosure Guidelines,* Disclosure Working Group, Edmonton, AB (Canadian Patient Safety Institute, 2008).

71. *Canadian Disclosure Guidelines* (Canadian Patient Safety Institute, 2008), 23.

72. For an excellent analysis of apology law in Canada, see Tracey M. Bailey, Elizabeth C. Robertson, and Gergely Hegedus, "Erecting Legal Barriers: New Apology Laws in Canada and the Patient Safety Movement: Useful Legislation or a Misguided Approach," *Health Law in Canada* 28, 2 (November 2007): 33–38.

Glossary

Active listening. A process of communication whereby the listener must hear, understand, and reflect back to the speaker that he has been heard and understood.

Apology. A principled communication process involving taking responsibility, expression of remorse, and an offer of reparation from one party to another, followed by acceptance of the words of apology and restoration of the relationship.

Arbitration. "A private voluntary dispute resolution process where the parties to a dispute agree in writing to submit the dispute for binding resolution to a third party neutral, chosen by the parties." *(See note 11.)*

Attribution. A belief or hypothesis we form about the underlying motivation for our own behaviour and others' behaviour. Attributions can be positive or negative.

BATNA. A party's best alternative or course of action in the event of failure to negotiate settlement of a conflict.

Climate. The prevailing temper, attitude, and outlook of a dyad, group, or organization. There are two types of climates: defensive and supportive. *(See note 30.)*

Collaborative agenda. The process of creating a list of neutrally worded issues, reflective of underlying needs of parties in conflict. The creation of the agenda provides an equal opportunity to all parties to contribute to the contents of the agenda.

Communication. The sending and receiving of messages: verbal, written, or non-verbal.

Conflict. All words and actions involving an "expressed struggle between two or more interdependent parties arising from a real or perceived difference in needs or values." *(See note 39.)*

Consensus approach. The approach to conflict resolution that does not seek to resolve issues through determination of underlying interests and needs. Rather, parties seek the path of least resistance. The solution to the conflict simply reflects what the majority can live with. Consensus building is not a win-win but rather a lose-lose "solution."

Convening stage. The second stage of principled conflict resolution in which parties actively consider who will come to the meeting, where they will meet, when they will meet, how the meeting will be structured, and what ground rules will govern attendees' behaviour at the meeting.

Core group. A group of individuals within an organization who have the power, influence, and knowledge to become catalysts for change. *(See note 54.)*

Dialogue. [In the workplace context] "a sustained collective search for shared meaning through verbal exchange." *(See note 6.)*

Ego needs. Stem from a sense of value in the workplace, and a sense of core principles that satisfy and promote the advancement and status of the individual worker.

Face needs. There are two kinds of face needs. Positive face is the desire to belong, to have approval of others, and to be seen as a particular type of person. Negative face is the desire for autonomy, not to be coerced or imposed upon by others.

Interests. Interests of parties to conflict arise from the basic needs of all human beings: physiological, safety, social connection, the need to be held in esteem, and the capacity to realize life goals (Maslow's Hierarchy of Needs).

Litigation. "An involuntary, formal, public process for dispute resolution, where a judge and/or jury determine facts, decrees and outcome to legal causes of action based on adversarial presentations by each party." *(See note 12.)*

Mediation. "A private voluntary dispute-resolution process in which a third party neutral, invited by all the parties, assists the parties in identifying issues of mutual concern, developing options for resolving those issues and finding resolutions acceptable to all parties." *(See note 10.)*

Negative attribution. The often incorrect conclusion that we form about others in which we assume they have bad intentions in their interactions with us.

Negotiation. A voluntary process involving direct dialogue between the parties in conflict, with no independent third party involved.

Position. Reflects the final desire or hoped-for solution of each party. It is generally not useful as a tool of communication.

Principled communication. (Also known as principled negotiation.) The process of seeking to understand the underlying interests of ourselves and those with whom we wish to interact. In the context of conflict, the process seeks to discover areas of *common* interests and needs of parties to the conflict, followed by brainstorming of options that address those common interests and needs—the "win-win."

Principled negotiation. A user-friendly inexpensive communication process for parties in conflict developed by Harvard professors Roger Fisher, William Ury, and Bruce Patton. The five steps involved are:

- Preparing to meet

- Convening the meeting

- Creating a collaborative agenda

- Identifying common interests

- Brainstorming solutions for mutual gain

Reframe. A process of restating a problem or position in a conflict in neutral language that is reflective of parties' underlying interests or needs.

Self-fulfillment needs. Stem from a desire for a sense of empowerment and creativity that allows people to achieve as individuals.

Shared meaning. To develop an understanding of issues in order to create options for resolving conflicts focusing on joint mutual gain.

Index

Bold numbers indicate illustrations.

About the Authors

Heather A. Lamoureux

Heather Lamoureux graduated from the Faculty of Law, University of Alberta, with distinction in 1975. From 1975 to 1995 she practised in the field of Civil Litigation primarily medical negligence and serious personal injury. In 1990 she received a Queen's Counsel Appointment and in 1995 was appointed to the Provincial Court of Alberta Criminal Division.

In 2003 Judge Lamoureux concluded a Masters Degree in Law at Pepperdine University, Los Angeles, California. Judge Lamoureux is an adjunct assistant professor in the Faculty of Medicine, University of Calgary. She is engaged in research, teaching, and writing in the field of conflict resolution in healthcare while continuing to sit as a full time judge in the Criminal Division. ■

Elaine D. Seifert, Q.C., B.A., LL.B. and LL.M

Elaine Seifert, Q.C., is a lawyer and specialist in dispute resolution. She was called to the Alberta Bar in 1988 and since 2003 she has practised exclusively in the areas of mediation, negotiation, arbitration, conflict management, and collaborative practice.

In addition to her dispute resolution practice, Elaine is an adjunct professor at the Faculty of Medicine, University of Calgary, where she, along with Judge Heather Lamoureux, teach a course to post graduate medical students on Resolving Conflict and Improving Communication. Elaine is also a sessional instructor at the Faculty of Law, University of Calgary.

Elaine had been an instructor with the Alberta Arbitration and Mediation Society since 2003, teaching Critical Skills for Conflict Resolution, Shifting from Positions to Interests, Resolving Interpersonal Conflict, and Mediation and Negotiation. ■